TWO GENERATIONS

A memoir of secrets, forgiveness and my father

ANNE CONNOR

IMPACT PRESS

First published in 2018 by Impact Press
an imprint of Ventura Press
PO Box 780, Edgecliff NSW 2027 Australia
www.impactpress.com.au

10 9 8 7 6 5 4 3 2 1

National Library of Australia Cataloguing-in-Publication entry:

Connor, Anne.
Two generations: a memoir of secrets, forgiveness and my father /
Anne Connor.

ISBN: 978-1-925384-41-3 (paperback)
ISBN: 978-1-925384-42-0 (ebook)

Cover and internal design: Deborah Parry
Cover images: Anne Connor

For Bernie, Scarlett, Jock and Bess – with gratitude and love.

CONTENTS

It can take six generations for suffering to work its way out of a family.

ANON

PREFACE

BASED ON TRUE EVENTS and told from a daughter's perspective, *Two Generations* alternates between reflection and dramatised reconstruction. Name changes and fictionalised characters and events have been introduced.

During the Second World War, Jock Connor served in Darwin and Lae, New Guinea where he became involved in a tragic accident with ramifications that resonated within my family, but were not spoken of.

My father's life is not complete without my mother. Affected too by this secret, was her collusion with him a way of protecting her husband and children? Together, they built their life and raised their family.

It is yet to play out how many generations will be affected.

INTRODUCTION

MY FATHER YELLED AT ME, 'Come back here and close that door quietly.'

I placed my hand on the door handle and slid the door on its worn runners until it made the slight thud it always made against the doorjamb. Still too loud. He pulled the door wide open, making a clunking sound when it stopped. 'Close it again and don't slam it.'

'It didn't slam.' My voice was shaky and weak.

He leaned his face closer to mine. 'Don't talk back. Close it.' I blinked away the burning tears and slipped my hand through the handle again and moved the door until it was nearly closed, then paused and eased it against the doorjamb.

Blood pounding in my head deafened me.

My father yanked the door wide open one more time. 'Close it.' Shaking, I slipped my hand through the handle that made it harder to control the door – but, at last, success.

No sound. I thought he'd be happy.

But once more, he pulled the door wide open. 'And again.'

By this time, more sensitive to the door's movement on its runners, I closed it in one hushed movement.

'Don't ever slam it again, do you hear me?'

I stared up at him. Stop yelling, I begged him under my breath.

'Did you hear what I said?' He leaned over me again, 'Answer me.'

'No. I mean yes, I won't slam it again, ever.' Ever, ever, ever.

His cheeks flushed and his chest moved with his breathing. He turned and walked back to the lounge room where he flopped back into his chair with a loud sigh. I tiptoed to my bedroom, curled up on my bed and cried.

My father's reaction to unexpected and loud noises confused and frightened me. Inexplicable, no-one ever spoke of it. Two decades after he died, I delved into his past and finally understood.

PROLOGUE

Lae, New Guinea, December 1943

HE COULD SMELL ANTISEPTIC. Blood and bits of flesh and splintered bone still covered his face and throat, his ruined army shirt. He sat on the edge of the bed next to timber trestle tables neatly laid with surgical dressings and medical instruments. Stretcher after stretcher of bandaged and bloodied soldiers lined both sides of the long tent. Men moaned, a few cried. Rain hammered the canvas roof.

He rested his elbows on his knees, leaned over and vomited. A beanpole of a medic materialised with a metal dish, too late. Regurgitated bully beef and bile soaked into the steamy, stinky mud. The soldier tried to stand, 'Joe,' he cried. His legs buckled, landing him in the muck. He curled up there and wept.

Another medic appeared and the two men tried to lift the soldier back onto the stretcher.

'Come on mate, lie down?'

'No, no, no, can't ...' Arms and legs stiffened. He lashed out, hitting both medics. Spit landed on the taller man's chin. 'Let me go, let me go.'

'Settle down mate, doc will be here soon.'

The soldier continued thrashing until a sharp jab stabbed his right arm.

PARENTS

1929

My father

LURED BY IMAGES OF Australia as a warm and sunny paradise, Jock Connor booked his ticket on the *Hobson's Bay*.

Posters showing verdant fruit blocks in Victoria's northern town of Mildura, orange trees groaning under an abundance of juicy ripe fruit, enticed the emigrants to leave their grey, bleak cities such as Manchester, where Jock lived; their meagre existence of two and three families living together in cramped rooms on streets of similar two-storey, poky houses built jammed up next to one another, backyards with an outside loo and not much else.

The brochures showed miles and miles of space, and just one house built on a quarter acre block; room for children to chase one another or for adults to grow vegetables and fruit trees in a climate of never-ending sunshine and mild winters. Compelled by the promise, the English filled migrant ships over and over again.

He caught a train to Southampton followed by a bus to the dock.

Passengers crammed onto the *Hobson's Bay* and craned at the ship's railing to catch the last glimpse of loved ones. Streamers flew as seamen pulled up anchor. The vessel slid away. Now inky water lapped against its sides and the ship's horn sounded giving everyone a start. As the streamers snapped one by one, people on water and land rummaged in handbags or pockets for handkerchiefs to wave in the breeze.

As he watched people farewelling their loved ones, Jock thought of the bleak scene with his mother that morning. The memory haunted him no matter how hard he tried to suppress it. A light knock at first, then louder. He waited a moment more before opening the bedroom door into the darkened room with its musty odour from the damp walls. She was still in the double bed she shared with the two youngest, now downstairs, up and dressed; ready to walk their big brother to the train station. Jock had five younger siblings, Marie, Mona, Ivy, Alf and Jack, still at home. The three older girls Ada, Anne and Nelly had married and lived elsewhere.

'I'm on my way now, Mother.'

She turned to the wall, pulling the blanket over her head.

'I'll write,' he said. 'As soon as I arrive, I'll write.'

She didn't move.

Please turn over. Please look at me, he thought and tried again.

'I'm off now, Mother, I'll write.' He waited at the door for a few moments, willing her to turn around, get out of bed, come and put her arms around him, kiss him on the cheek and say, 'I love you son, have a great trip.'

'Goodbye now, Mother.' He gently closed the door behind him, careful not to make a noise, stood in the darkened hallway and blinked away tears, not wanting his brothers and sisters witnessing such weakness.

My mother told me this story during my growing years; it didn't come from him. When I heard this I thought my grandmother Ada to be a hard, emotionless woman. But as I grew older and became a mother myself I empathised with the grief she must have experienced losing her eldest son to the other side of the world and not knowing whether she'd ever see him again. For years, Jock had been the major breadwinner in the family as Ada had lost her husband in an accident at work a decade earlier. How fearful she must have been, wondering what the future might hold for her and the other children without him. What a wretched scene; a mother and son's sadness and the inexpressible chasm between them.

He picked up the old suitcase Elsie, his neighbour, had given him and left the house.

Mona, Ivy and Jack walked him to the train station and stood on the platform waving. He watched as they became smaller and smaller until the train chugged around a corner and they disappeared.

He kept his coat buttoned so his improvised belt, an old tie, stayed hidden. The jacket had belonged to his father – a meagre inheritance. Worn at the elbows, frayed on the cuffs and collar, it had seen better days. He'd folded newspaper into the bottom of his shoes, something between the ground and his threadbare socks.

As the *Hobson's Bay* slipped away from the dock, Jock leaned on the rail and watched seagulls diving into the choppy waves. An onlooker might have thought him older than his twenty-three years. He had bright blue eyes and a frown between his eyebrows that obscured a childhood scar. Robust, but thin and wiry, he had worked as an adult while still a child.

For years, he'd thought of leaving England. He yearned for a richer, warmer life where the sun shone for days at a time. The dank poverty of his existence was unbearable. With no other prospects, his quest turned to Australia. He dared hope for a better life for himself, even marry and have children. His mother and siblings might even follow. Then she'd know he'd made the right choice in leaving, and the dull sensation in the pit of his stomach every time he thought of her, might leave him for good.

He looked back and Southampton appeared as a speck on the

horizon. He hadn't banked on feeling so alone. The sense of the impending departure had kept him going during the last long English winter. Now his dream had become a reality, his thoughts kept landing in a very different place.

I must be a miserable sod; no-one to see me off this end and no-one at the other.

My mother

BESSIE BROWN GREW UP on a farm in Balliang near Geelong in Victoria. When she told me stories of her past, she described the house the same every time.

My grandfather Tom had built their small cottage from planks of raw wood nailed together with a floor of rough timber. Rusted iron sheets formed the makeshift roof, which leaked in heavy downpours. Discarded kerosene tins and small logs littered a sloping veranda – tacked on as an afterthought. To close the front door, Bess had to lift and shove it in one movement. Gaps at the top and bottom allowed hot or cold winds to blow through the house, depending on the season. Three windows at the rear mirrored three at the front. Scrubby trees grew on either side of the house and a corroded iron gate leaned against a dead bush.

Inside was dark. Pots and pans hanging from nails hammered into the walls created a dim halo over a black woodstove. To the left sat a table and six chairs. To the right, a bench forever covered in flour. Hessian curtains my grandmother Mary had sewed from sugar bags hung at the windows.

Two bedrooms ran off to the left, one with an iron double bed where my grandparents slept, the second furnished with four single beds, pushed together for my mother and her siblings.

Tom left his loaded guns by the front door.

From the age of six, Bess milked cows before school. Winters were the worst. By the light of a kerosene lamp, she slipped on her clothes and boots before traipsing through the mud to the milking sheds, her face and fingers stinging from the icy wind. She'd place her rickety wooden stool next to the milker, close her eyes, lean her forehead against the cow's warm side and rub her hands across its flank in an effort to bring circulation back into her numb fingers. She squeezed and pulled the heavy teats in rhythm with the dull sound of milk squirting into the metal bucket.

At sundown, Mary heated scrubbed rocks in the wood stove before wrapping them in cloth to make a warm parcel for each child's bed. In the mornings, she made breakfast and carried large wooden trays piled with plates of eggs, bacon and toasted homemade bread to men employed on the farm. They came looking for food and board for a fair day's work and built their own sleeping quarters – a lean-to attached to the milking shed – from kerosene tins hammered flat, timber and hessian bags.

During the sweltering summers, Mary's spirit dwindled as the north winds stripped the last drop of moisture from the ground, causing it to crack right open. Stands of eucalyptus dotted about the paddocks offered the cattle and sheep little shelter from the relentless sun. For miles parched land shimmered in the heat haze. A dam in the western paddock, the main water supply for grazing animals, too often dried to a puddle of sludge breeding swarms of mosquitoes. Livestock, wading too far in for relief, became bogged in the slurry and died a slow death, their bloated bodies half-sunk in the mud. Tom towed the ones he could to safety by wrapping one end of a rope around the horn of his saddle, the other encircling the cow's middle.

Life on the land was bleak in the early nineteen-hundreds. Mary had four babies in eight years; my mother Elizabeth, or Bess, then Frank, Honor and Tilly. Left weaker after each baby's arrival, Mary became thin and drawn, her complexion sallow. Grey-streaked tendrils from her pinned-up hair fell over her face.

To stop the ravages of the Australian sun during the long hot summers, Mary always wore a straw hat outdoors. Blowflies swarmed over food during the meals' preparation. They hovered over dinner plates set at the table and landed on food caked on the babies' faces. Tom had migrated from Ireland. Under the Australian sun, his face burned, peeled and burned again until he bought himself a wide-brimmed hat from Geelong's general store. He wore his tweed jacket buttoned-up in winter and worked with his shirtsleeves rolled up in the scorching summer.

As Bess and her siblings grew and helped around the farm, Mary's strength improved. She enjoyed the in-between seasons – spring and autumn. At these times, Mary took the children on walks through the scrub and for picnics by the dam. Sandwiches with bread filled with sliced ham from one of their own pigs were cut, and lemons squeezed to make sugary lemonade. Mary wrapped lunch in a tablecloth she had embroidered with little girls in bonnets and long dresses, placing the food in a wicker basket.

At the weir, Mary stretched out, under gum trees, on eiderdowns pulled from the children's beds. The high sun's rays filtered through the leaves, so different from the punishing summer sun. During these times, Bess noticed her mother's spirit lift. Mary appeared at peace breathing in the bush smells and soft air as gentle breezes wafted up the valley.

The children loved to play hide-and-seek. Mary spread out face down, on an eiderdown, with her forehead resting on her crossed arms and counted in a loud voice while the children scattered.

'One hundred. Coming, ready or not.'

She pretended she didn't know where they were and wandered

around saying, 'I wonder where those children are. They must be somewhere. I hope they haven't gone too far.'

When the sport had run its course, the youngsters ran off to explore the bush, leaving their mother to rest in the benign sun, watching clouds scudding across the blue sky.

Bess loved horses. She hadn't long turned twelve the day she noticed a young stallion standing in the middle of the breaking-in yard. Not yet fully grown, he was more than a colt, and chestnut brown with a white diamond on his forehead. She slipped under the railing and he backed off a few steps.

'Hello, boy. You're mighty handsome,' she whispered. She recognised the signs of a brumby on full alert: eyes wide, ears flat, head high, breathing heavily. She stood still, holding her hand out, palm upwards. He raced off, raising a cloud of dust behind him. She took her time stepping backwards, not taking her eyes off him. Resting her elbows on the top of the railing, her chin cupped in her hands, she gazed at the steed; such a beauty.

Each day before and after school, she visited him with a handful of hay dipped in molasses. He approached sniffing the sweet, pungent offering. His warm breath and his raspy tongue made her smile. She called him Brown Horse and stroked his sweaty neck. At first, he flinched, his muscles tensed, before he shook his head and settled.

She softened her voice. 'We can be mates. I won't hurt you.'

The whiff of feed and molasses lingered as she slipped through the fence.

In time, he moved towards her, a small step, and allowed her to rub his velvety nose as he ate the sticky fodder and licked her hand clean. One day, she held the bridle close to his face. He inhaled and pulled back.

'I won't hurt you, cobber.'

The next day, she moved closer, slipped the leather over his face and buckled the halter behind his ears, then led him around the enclosure, her voice calm and quiet. It wasn't long before Bess realised he trusted her. In class she gazed out the window daydreaming of riding the brumby. She rushed home, leaving her sisters and brother dawdling along the track, and sprinted past the house on her way to the breaking-in yard – she froze. The stench of fresh horse manure filled the air. Her father was thrashing Brown Horse's hindquarters with his pigskin crop while the foreman pulled hard on a rope tied around the young stallion's neck. The brumby's ears stayed pinned back flat, his eyes open wide. She wanted to yell, Stop, please stop. But knew such insolence might cause her father to turn the whip on her.

That night she lay awake in her bed until her siblings had fallen asleep. She waited for absolute silence from her parent's room, crept out from under her blankets, wrapped her eiderdown around her and snuck through the house and out the back door. She lit the lamp and tiptoed to the stables, pulled a bunch of hay from the bale, scooped a handful of molasses from the drum and rubbed it through the dry feed. Brown Horse stomped the ground.

Bess clicked her tongue, 'Come on. It's alright. I won't hurt you.' Eventually, he hung his head and sauntered over to smell the food. In the weak lamplight, she saw dried blood on his neck. She gently touched the welts while he ate his midnight feast and she wiped her tears and runny nose on the quilt.

It was the spring lamb sale in Ballarat, and farmers travelled to town to bid for stock. With Tom away, Bess wanted Brown Horse broken-in, her way, without her father's brutal force.

A gentler rhythm resonated in the home during Tom's absence. Mary hummed as she busied herself with her daily chores, and did not interfere when her daughter spent every spare moment with the brumby, leading him around the enclosure; one day slipping a blanket over his back; the next day, two rugs; the next day three. On the fourth, she threw on a saddle. He flinched at first, his shoulders and hindquarters twitching against the rough wool on his skin. It didn't take long for him to settle. The stirrups jangled either side of his great belly and he nuzzled her hair as she led him.

She found it difficult to sleep that night. The following day she had planned to ride Brown Horse. She hoped he'd cooperate with her in the saddle. She rushed home from school and went through her ritual: she fed him the sweetened hay and placed the bridle on his face, talking while she did so, 'That's my boy, good boy.'

Bessie threw the blanket on his back, followed by the saddle, tightened the strap under his middle and let the stirrups drop either side. As she put one foot in the ring, his body tensed. She stroked his neck and rubbed his chest. 'There, there, it's alright.' She positioned all her weight on the stirrup and with a slight jump she was up. Tall and strong from daily physical work on the farm, Bess had been riding horses half her life. She held the reins tight. Brown Horse flinched, walked backwards, circled and eventually stood still.

His neck felt warm and relaxed; she nudged him with her knees and he broke into a trot.

Then her father returned. Bess ran into the house and saw him sitting at the table. Time away had mellowed his mood. He was handing out humbugs. Bessie sucked on the boiled sweet as her da leaned back in his chair. He was smiling; she could tell he'd had a good time. She parked the humbug against the inside of her cheek.

'Can I give you a hand with the jinker, Father?'

'That's a fine thing to say, let's do it together.'

Father and daughter stood either side of the sweaty grey. Bess undid one section of the harness while her father loosened the other.

'Father, I have a surprise for you.'

'A surprise!'

'I've been working with the brown brumby and he let me ride him.'

Bess heard the gravel crunch under his boots. She fiddled with the buckles on the horse's rein, not daring to look up. He loomed over her. 'You stupid girl, I've told you not to go near those wild horses. They're killers. Look at me when I speak to you.'

She turned her eyes slowly to meet his. She knew she was entering dangerous territory. 'He's very gentle.'

Tom's cheeks flushed. Dirt and sweat packed the creases of his forehead. He smelled of stale sweat and the sweetness of humbugs.

She softened her voice. 'I'll show you.' She ran to the barn, picked up the saddle, bridle and blanket, then walked slowly towards Brown Horse. As she slid through the fence rails, the brumby raised his head and moved towards her, slowly at first before quickening his pace.

'Hello, boy.' She patted under his chin and rubbed her nose against his. She ran her hands along his side and flank, threw on the rug and saddle and was up on his back in a flash. With a gentle squeeze of her knees, Brown Horse sauntered around the enclosure.

Her father watched as his daughter took the brumby through basic drills, walking, trotting, walking again. Rider and mount performed well. Bess was happy and proud at what she and her horse had achieved. She bent over and hugged his neck, looked up to catch her father's eye and smiled. Tom turned on his heel and strode towards the house.

That night a heavy silence fell on the family. Bess wished her mother would hum again.

Farming is seasonal and at times Tom hired extra men to help out with the milking. At these times, it was Bess and Honor's job to help Mary cook breakfast. The two girls carried the heavy wooden tray between them, making sure not to slip in the mud. After that, Honor prepared the children's lunches while Bess harnessed the grey to the front of the jinker ready for the ride to school. With everyone on board, she'd flick the horse's rump and they'd take off out the wooden gates and along the long road to the track that led to the school. On the way, they'd pick up the neighbour's children, Joanie and Nugget Higgins.

The school was just one room. Long wooden tables and benches sat in rows and a blackboard on wheels stood at the front. Eleven students aged between five and twelve shared the room with one teacher, Mr Hardfish, who lived on his own on the premises. Tall, thin and stooped, he had a beard flecked with remnants from his last meal. While the teacher had taken a shine to Bess, he picked on her little brother Frank, who found it difficult to concentrate in class and soon became distracted. Hardfish handed out unwarranted beatings to Frank. Bess tried to sit next to her brother to help him understand Hardfish's instructions. The teacher's intentions towards Bess were inappropriate. He'd lean in too close and place his hand on her shoulder while he took her through the work. Bess didn't feel she had the right to complain or to tell her parents, so she tolerated his touching. At least he is not thrashing Frank, she thought.

SECRETS

Anzac Day 1991

WE HAD NOT LONG returned from North Fitzroy's Edinburgh Gardens where my eighteen-month-old daughter and I skipped through dinner-plate autumn leaves. Distracted by a sound on the front porch, I opened the door to find my brother Galvin, pale and upset.

The two of us sat on the couch in our front room. With my daughter on my lap, I sniffed lavender shampoo as I nuzzled the back of her head. A motorbike sped up the side street. Lace curtains billowed in the mid-afternoon breeze.

My brother had attended an Anzac Day gathering earlier in the day, representing our father who had died almost two decades earlier. He had contacted Ron Jackson, a warm and open-hearted man who had known Dad, who welcomed my brother and introduced him to members of Dad's regiment, the 2/14th Australian Field Regiment.

That's when it happened, one of those life-is-different-now moments. An old man from Dad's regiment told my brother of a tragic incident my father had been involved in. The information so disturbed Galvin he still finds it difficult to discuss. Was it an unguarded comment from the old soldier? Maybe it was the shock of seeing Jock's son who strongly resembles his father; whatever the reason, nearly twenty years after my father's death, his terrible war secret was revealed.

But the details died with him and the people he knew. I needed to know more.

My father had marched in Anzac Day parades. Not owning a car, he phoned one of his army mates the night before to organise a lift. Failing that, he'd catch the train into Melbourne. One year when the commemoration was televised, my sister, brothers and I gathered in the lounge room around the black-and-white television housed in a solid red teak box. The men looked proud. Bony bodies had filled out; waists had thickened; double-breasted suits replaced army uniforms. They smiled with medals pinned over their hearts on pinstriped lapels, no doubt pleased to see one another. An affection and respect remained between them no matter how many years had passed. People lined the streets of Melbourne and waved tiny Australian flags to honour their returned soldiers.

The parade seemed to go for hours and, bored by the monotony of it, I stretched out on the floor and filled a new colouring-in book. I sharpened my pencils many times while group after group of men, military jeeps, army, navy and community bands appeared on the screen. Two men carrying banners walked in front of each cluster, bearing the emblem identifying the division and company. Then the pennant of Dad's regiment came into view, egg-shaped with a perpendicular line across it.

'Mum! Quick, Dad might be on,' my brother yelled.

Mum hurried into the lounge room, wiping her hands on the bottom of her apron. She walked up to the screen and squinted, still wringing her apron between her fingers, even though her hands were dry.

'I think you're right,' she said. 'It's him. Look at that.'

We all peered closer. I was kneeling with my nose only inches from the screen. And there was Dad's head and shoulders in a sea of marchers. He was smiling, and in three seconds he was gone and replaced by another banner followed by another group of men.

Mum walked back into the kitchen saying over her shoulder, 'Switch it off now and go outside and play. Too nice to be inside.'

Watching television in the daytime was an unusual thing for us to do. Generally, it wasn't allowed and we needed permission to turn on the box. Watching our father in the Anzac Day march was a special occasion.

My brother pressed the fat knob on the side of the teak box and the screen faded to pale grey with just a black dot in the centre until that too disappeared. The room seemed empty without the music of the military bands and the excitement of anticipating and seeing our father. I went back to my colouring-in. It seemed strange to see Dad on television marching with a group of strangers. I couldn't imagine him having a life outside our family.

In the late 1960s, a shift in thinking crept into Australia's collective consciousness. As a preoccupied adolescent, I wasn't much interested in what was going on in the world. I wasn't listening and there wasn't the bombardment of media that we live with today. In my family, we weren't encouraged to discuss politics or what was happening in the world. Though, I do remember protesters against the Vietnam War rallying in the streets, and the returning veterans being shunned. They were embarrassed to have served, even though for many their fate was sealed when a politician thrust his hand into a barrel and pulled out a marble with their birthdate on it. Many grew their hair long and made their escape in recreational drugs or alcohol.

Crowds attending Anzac Day gatherings diminished until only a handful of straggling bystanders remained and the ranks of marchers thinned. One year, Melbourne's Shrine of Remembrance was defaced with the word 'PEACE!' painted in large white letters on the pillars of the north portico. Due to the porous nature of the stone, the slogan remained visible for more than twenty years. Spokesmen on behalf of war veterans and their families were apoplectic and called for the culprits to be caught and strung up. I thought I remembered the pine trees along Ceremonial Drive being cut down by demonstrators around the same time, but I could find no record of it. The Shrine's online history section couldn't help. I emailed their enquiries page and didn't receive a response. I looked through *The Age* archives online and couldn't find any entry there either. Maybe I imagined it.

The war against war was intense and I became one of these people. During Melbourne's Moratorium against the Vietnam War in the winter of 1971, close to 100,000 people demonstrated, closing the centre of Melbourne. As a teenager, I began to take notice and was influenced by the people I mixed with. I didn't demonstrate, but quietly disagreed with Anzac Day and what it represented.

After I had left home and started a family of my own, my brothers took my mother to what was called the 'bombing lunch'. Scheduled on the anniversary of the first bombing of Darwin, men from Dad's regiment and their families attended these gatherings. My father had died and Mum looked forward to these get-togethers enormously. I imagine she found comfort talking to men who had known her husband. She often suggested I should join them as I would enjoy it.

'They make such a fuss, love,' she said.

I declined. I didn't want to push my anti-war sentiment, but I did not want to be involved.

I regret the years when I squandered the opportunity to meet and talk with men who are now no longer with us, who had known my father. I missed out on finding out more about the man whose DNA I share. My judgements had kept me from finding a richer story.

In those years, I was unaware of what the soldiers in Darwin had experienced. I had not known the extent of the attacks on what was then a little-known town. How men who were sent there were under-resourced, unsupported and unprepared. Many Australians are still unaware of what took place in Darwin. It has been a well-kept secret. If I had known then what I know now, I would gladly have attended those lunches. I hadn't realised soldiers in Darwin were armed with leftover guns from the First World War with little ammunition. Modern artillery had been allocated to members of the armed forces shipped overseas to support Britain in its war against Germany, leaving combatants to defend Australia with outdated and inadequate guns. These firearms were not calibrated for the tropics so were close to useless. As ammunition ran out, soldiers were supplied with sharpened star pickets against an airborne enemy.

My brothers also encouraged me to be there. 'There are some great characters there. You'd really like it.'

They were annoyed when I responded, 'Why would I enjoy gathering with a bunch of strangers to commemorate killing people?'

But over time my stance on Anzac Day commemorations began to soften. I can't pinpoint the actual reason or the time when I began to think differently. Maybe it was maturity, maybe it was curiosity. Perhaps, I had been influenced by the groundswell of new-found respect for returned veterans. Or perhaps, it was a combination of all of these things. The seed for this book was beginning to germinate and I wanted to see, meet and talk to those who had known my father to gain more insight into his story. A few years ago, I did attend an Anzac Day parade and walked with the ten or so remaining men from my father's regiment. These old gentlemen had tears in their eyes when they met me. 'I remember Jock very well,' said a man called Vin.

'He was a great man,' said Linc.

'Always had a joke to tell,' said Ron.

Linc chimed in again, 'Played the spoons, didn't he?'

'Yes, he did,' I said, picturing Dad holding the spoons between his middle fingers and clicking them together as he moved his hands in swift circles. It had seemed impossibly deft to me as a child.

These men had stood side-by-side with my father. They had known him better than I did before he was the man who became my dad. They stood in the Melbourne autumn air smiling, happy, grateful, humble and very pleased to meet me. My judgements fell away with every line-etched hand I shook. My superiority dwindled when people of all ages, young parents with children in prams, well-dressed young women and men and teenagers clapped as we passed. Many called out their thanks as we walked along St Kilda Road to Melbourne's Shrine of Remembrance.

To say I felt quite embarrassed about my stance against commemorating the war is an understatement. I understood this now. This was not the exaltation of war. This was gratitude. This was sadness for the waste of life, for the war scars my father's generation lived with. This was good mates seeing one another again as they had done for over seventy years; such friendships were born out of horrific circumstances.

Of course, there is still that idealised conception of war that Alec Campbell, the last First World War veteran so poignantly reminded us of on his deathbed, 'For God's sake, don't glorify Gallipoli – it was a terrible fiasco, a total failure and best forgotten.' This glorification is what I had unconsciously rejected and reflected even in the way sports' commentators use words such as conflict, battle and glory to call the Anzac Day football match. An industry has been built upon hero-worshipping the Anzacs from that curious oxymoron the Great War and returned soldiers from the wars that followed. But it is an insubstantial worship, as American writer Chris Hedges observes in *Death of the Liberal Class*:

The wounded, the crippled, and the dead are, in this great charade, swiftly carted off stage. They are war's refuse. We do not see them. We do not hear them. They are doomed, like wandering spirits, to float around the edges of our consciousness, ignored, even reviled. The message they tell is too painful for us to hear. We prefer to celebrate ourselves and our nation by imbibing the myths of glory, honour, patriotism, and heroism, words that in combat become empty and meaningless.[1]

My new-found experience of Anzac Day was quite different from either polarity. I saw the annual coming-together as people taking part in a ritual of death and life. That remembering is about respecting and having gratitude for people who had no control over the adversity they faced, but who maintained a belief that what they did was right, was for the better and would contribute to a more peaceful world. It is about remembering with gratefulness those who died defending our country.

1 From *Death of the Liberal Class* by Chris Hedges, © 2010. Reprinted by permission of Nation Books, an imprint of Hachette Book Group, Inc.

BEFORE THE WAR

*My father seldom spoke of the war, but he spoke of his time in
Darwin before the bombing in 1942. What another world for him.
The searing heat, stifling humidity, perpetual heavy downpours,
mosquitoes, open space and red dirt. When I helped Mum organise
his things after he died, I found old composition books where he had
written, in scratchy pencil, information on Darwin and snippets
of conversations he'd had.*

HE'D SHOWN A KEEN interest in how the town became settled
and had searched for people to tell him of its history. He'd saved old
newspaper articles about life in Darwin prior to white man's arrival,
Chinatown and the town's personalities.

One newspaper commentary featured the Larrakia people who
had inhabited Darwin sixty thousand years ago. In the 1700s,
they traded with the Macassans, who sailed from the south-east
of the Celebes. In exchange for fishing rights to the trepang, or
sea cucumber – a slug-like creature that lived on the seabed –
the Larrakia received knives, cloth, rice, tobacco and alcohol.
The Macassans fished for trepang at low tide, by hand, spearing,

diving or dredging. Placed in boiling water before being dried and smoked, preserved the catch for the journey back to Makassar and other South-East Asian markets. Trepang became valued for its gelatinous texture, its flavour-enhancing properties, plus its use as a stimulant and aphrodisiac.

It is believed Lieutenant John Lort Stokes of the HMS *Beagle* was the first person to see Darwin. In 1839, Commander John Clements Wickham named the port after Charles Darwin, the British naturalist who had sailed with them on earlier expeditions. Thirty years later, George Goyder the Surveyor-General of South Australia established a small settlement of one hundred and thirty-five people. Erecting the first poles for the Overland Telegraph connected Australia to the rest of the world. The discovery of gold at Pine Creek in the 1880s further boosted the young colony's development. Darwin became the settlement's official name in 1911, on its transfer to the federal administration.

Jock had written notes describing life in Darwin in the 1920s. My research enabled me to expand on his records. Archival material described a sleepy complacent shantytown, untidy and sprawling. Doors and windows were left open and robberies non-existent. Many families lived in tents and buildings made of fibro or hessian. While racially tolerant, with the Larrakia people, Japanese, Chinese, Malay, Philippinos and Europeans living peacefully together, Darwin remained a segregated town. Anglo-Saxons lived in Smith and Mitchell Streets and the Esplanade. Cavanagh Street became Chinatown and Aboriginals stayed at the compound or the police paddock, known as Stuart Park.

Children fell asleep to an orchestra of sound: Aboriginals singing and clacking their bilma by the racecourse creek; frogs croaking, mopokes hooting, insects whirring and buzzing. Dingoes howling around herds of goats, waiting to snatch a straying kid – goats were hardier than sheep and the milk became a valuable commodity. Children milked the goats and cleaned the bottles before school by scrubbing the glass flasks with a bottlebrush and tipping a handful of pebbles into the neck of the container. The children made a game of it, rattling the stones around and around until the dried milk scum coated the grits. They rinsed the bottles before boiling them on an old wood stove that never went out. Aboriginal boys kept the wood boxes filled and fires stoked. Once sterilised and dried, warm, frothy milk was poured into bottles before being corked and sold to the locals for a shilling.

For the ambitious, opportunities were plenty. Cavanagh Street's Chinatown began with a few modest humpies where staple vegetables and fruit from the local Chinese market gardens were sold. As businesses prospered, dwellings grew to residences and cafes. Ming Loong owned a large general store – Fang Chong Loong – in a long double-storey building with verandas top and bottom.

Chinese boys who worked for Ming left their two-wheelers leaning against the railing, when not delivering groceries. Bikes soon became a favourite method of transport with only a few cars yet in the town. Buildings in the precinct spread by being tacked together with available materials such as corrugated iron, tin or hessian. Joss sticks and ornate dragon doors decorated the entrance to Fang Chong Loong's store. Stocked shelves contained colourful and mysterious merchandise: Chinese dolls, clothing, strange-looking and smelling herbs and camphor wooden boxes. Pleasant and approachable, Ming made friends with everyone in town; sometimes the men invited him home for a beer. At just four foot ten, with his plaited ponytail hanging to his waist, he cut a colourful sight drinking with the locals. He wore loose pants, elasticised at the ankle, a long tunic and walked with short rushed steps in his black canvas slippers.

At Christmas time, Ming had the Chinese boys deliver Christmas parcels to his customers' homes. Presents included striking, ornate wooden boxes, their tasselled lids covered in silk fabric of dragons and birds. Sweet-smelling, delicious dark chocolates filled two drawers in the same vibrant cloth, an exotic gift for the people of Darwin.

Ming's wife Zhou and the other women of Chinatown had tiny feet and wore tiny shoes in which they shuffled along the wide dusty streets of frontier Darwin, a long way from old China where mothers broke daughters' toes and bound them as an act of love and protection. Zhou's mother had wrapped her young daughter's feet as a status symbol, a way for Zhou to marry into money. Ming and Zhou's daughters Cecelia and Margery came into the world in Darwin's first hospital; built out of old corrugated iron, the hospital perched above Doctor's Gully. When not at school or working in the market gardens or the shop, the girls ran barefoot on the beach with the Aboriginal and white kids, forging strong lifelong friendships.

In 1938, the Fong Lim family moved to Darwin and set up general stores, cafes, tailor shops, hotels and wholesaling in the Northern Territory. In 2013, when I visited Darwin for the seventy-first commemoration of the bombing, fifth generation Australian Katrina Fong Lim was Lord Mayor of the town. A welcoming, confident woman, Katrina embraced visitors and locals as old friends. Her ancestor, George Fong Lim, bought a store in the white part of Darwin, next to the open-air Star Theatre in Smith Street; it had a drapery on one side and milk bar and grocery store on the other.

'It won't succeed,' people said. 'No-one will patronise a Chinese business outside of Chinatown.' But he proved the critics wrong; the shop flourished. George began work at five in the morning and finished at midnight. George believed business had to be a family affair to succeed; his wife and their children all had their part to play. The boys delivered groceries on their bicycles and the girls served behind the counter or packaged foodstuffs out the back.

Two Japanese pearl-fishermen set up across the road from the Star Theatre. Records show them nameless – just the 'Japs who sold Jap squashes'. These glamorous drinks became something new to Darwin and for decades after, residents reminisced, 'Remember the Jap squashes?'

The owners made their own syrup, from a secret list of ingredients. A contraption with a sharp piece of steel at one end held a block of ice in place. It was then shaved with another piece of wood with nails hammered into one end. They shook the frosty scrapings and the secret syrup vigorously. When people attended the Star on Wednesday and Saturday evenings, the two men did a roaring business. People rushed out at interval to buy their squashes and ice-cream from the Japanese and home-roasted salted peanuts from George Fong Lim's son Alec, who sold them on the street outside the theatre.

For the people of Darwin, pictures at the Star, exotic Japanese drinks and fresh roasted peanuts made for special treats. Wednesday night the cinema opened for Aborigines only and Western movies played. On Saturday nights, Anglos attended and the latest movies featured. They dressed to the hilt, men in white linen suits and ladies in long frocks and straw hats with netting. Tickets to the outdoor theatre cost two and six each.

Tradesmen attracted by the district allowance and overtime earned in such a remote place made their way to Darwin. They constructed bungalows at Miley Point, the New Darwin Hotel, the Bank of New South Wales, the Commonwealth Savings Bank and the post office. Housing was built in a quasi-Asian style to accommodate Darwin's searing sticky heat and the monsoon rain and winds. The style evoked the tropics and was reminiscent of a long-distant colonial past many associated with leisure, pleasure and prosperity. Constructed on stilts, buildings had enclosed wide verandas around the top storey. With ceiling fans installed and louvre windows opened to let the breeze through or closed to keep out the harsh monsoon rains, people often slept on the verandas to gain the briefest of breezes on a hot night. Gauze wire kept insects at bay.

The two-storey New Darwin Hotel's colonial architecture and location on the Esplanade overlooking the Timor Sea proved popular with wealthy visitors and dignitaries. Business meetings often took place on the second storey balcony. Next door the post office was built at ground level with a wooden veranda at the front and a wire and post fence separating the building from the unmade footpath. This nondescript building became a busy meeting place for many of the townspeople, dropping off mail, picking up mail, sending and receiving telegrams.

Mr and Mrs Bald and their teenage daughter Iris took up residence at the post office and became popular in town. The Bald family became part of the town's tragic history.

Complacency was rife when the war started, as the war appeared a very long way from Darwin. But, by 1941, a carnival atmosphere had taken hold in the town. The arrival of the Darwin Mobile Force had increased the population. Streets were busy and the welcome sound of cash registers rang out. Canvas-covered army trucks filled with soldiers with time on their hands rolled through town and many of them wound up at the Gordon Don Hotel. I can't imagine Jock spending much time at the hotel. His alcohol consumption consisted of a shandy on a scorching summer's night. I imagine he spent most of his spare time writing letters home, playing cards or reading.

Jock's regiment was kept busy with constructing roads south to Adelaide River and Tennant Creek plus erecting steel poles for signals and telegraph wires. As one of the ninety-nine signalmen across a 373-mile distance, his crew set-up signal bases.

What a change it must have been for my father to find himself in northern Australia living in a dusty frontier town. Since his arrival on the Hobson's Bay just over a decade earlier, the world had changed for him and for the nation. His accent had changed. The flat Australian inflection started creeping into his speech. He wasn't the only one who was different; he noticed people around him had altered. When he docked in 1929, the Australians he met had open faces, were carefree, welcoming, trusting. Now, he observed faces etched with worry and fear.

On the day he had sailed into Melbourne in 1929, I can picture a young man on his own exiled from everything he knew. On the deck of the ship as it ploughs through dark water, he leans against the rail, as he did when he left Southampton weeks earlier. This time, he anticipates hellos, welcomes, new friends, a new life. I see him young, excited, faced with endless opportunities. His life filled with the excitement of the unknown. I wish I knew more of what he thought, experienced. What was it like to be displaced from familiar sights, smells, sounds? Had he thought of this, leading up to his departure? Or did the invincibility of youth drive his actions?

What I do know is when Jock sailed into Port Melbourne on that autumn day, the country had a population of over six million. People listened to thirty-thousand radios, spoke to one another on four hundred thousand telephones and drove five hundred thousand cars, making the country one of the top five nations in vehicle ownership.

Possibly, there was a chill in the air that day and I hope bright sunshine. I fancy when he walked down the gangplank, his last step may have been a small jump onto solid ground. Maybe, he clicked his heels together in mid-air.

Immigration processing took place in large corrugated iron sheds on the wharf. Jock wanted to make his way to the port town of Geelong where he knew the Valley Worsted Mill needed workers.

———————

The mill had been modelled on the factories in Lancashire. Except in Geelong the grey smoke wafted up and up into a high china blue sky, unlike the heavy grey sky in England forcing the fumes onto people, houses and streets.

Jock was offered a job, to start the next day working in the weaving room. He found lodgings at The Lord Nelson hotel and after unpacking Elsie's suitcase, he had a wash, sat at the wooden table and opened his diary. Every time he wrote, he remembered Mrs Dalton's words on the day his mother pulled him out of school. 'You're a clever lad Jock, may sure you read and write every day so you don't lose what you've been taught. A diary's a good way of keeping up your writing and this is a good start.' She handed him a leather-bound book of blank pages and a wooden box of pencils. He wrote:

13 APRIL 1929
Arrived at Port Melbourne, caught bus and train to Geelong this morning, found work at mill and lodgings at Lord Nelson. Geelong is a busy industrial town. Plenty of bikes, buses and cars. Kicks up lots of dust. Tomorrow start at mill and hope things not different to factories at home. People friendly. A few factories in other parts of town. Will write Mother letting her know her firstborn son is safe.

The mill's internal sections were identical to the ones in England, with a large weaving room filled with loud clunking, vibrating looms intertwining the weft and waft threads. Jock knew he had to ensure the looms didn't jam and threads didn't buckle and jar the machinery, and if they did, to mend them at once to keep them moving along. Then he'd lift the woven material into large crates on wheels.

Employment made it easier to find cheaper accommodation than the Lord Nelson. He bought a copy of the *Geelong Advertiser* and found an advertisement for a room in a boarding house a few streets away from the mill. This took place within a couple of weeks after his jump onto Australian ground. With his first pay, he bought himself a new pair of shoes and a second-hand bike, and he joined the throng of Geelong cyclists.

Jock visited the Free Library in his spare time and lapped up the opportunity to read as much as possible. He noticed the poster on the library's wall: *Easter Dance in the Corio Tennis Club Hall – the opening event of the social season.*

My mother told me she and Dad met at a dance in Geelong. What I do know is that he asked her for a dance and something began. I suppose many couples had their start on the dance floor; it must be a common story, but to me, it holds a mythic quality upon which hung the future. If I tried to turn their meeting and courtship into a story, based on the man and woman who became my parents, it would go like this.

Jock enters the dance hall and sees Bess, who is hovering by the supper table with two other girls. She's wearing a pale blue cotton knee-length frock; her dark-brown curly hair is cut short in the flapper-style of the day.

Jock waits and is rewarded when the object of his interest is left on her own. He walks over and taps Bess on the shoulder, and says, in the space of one breath, 'Hello, I'm Jock Connor. I was wondering whether you'd dance with me this evening.'

'You're not from around here,' she replies, evading the question. 'Haven't seen you before and I don't know anyone who speaks like that either. Where're you from?'

'Lancashire, England.'

'Well, Jock Connor from Lancashire, England, I'll tell you the way we do things here.' She smiles and waves the card she is holding. 'We ladies have dance cards and it's the blokes' job to ask girls to book a dance on their card.'

'What's your name then? You know my story.'

'Bess Brown. Family and friends call me Bessie.'

'And where are you from?'

'Well if you must know, Mr Sticky-beak, I live in Geelong, but I grew up on a farm at Balliang. We moved into town a couple of years ago.'

'Well, Bessie Brown from Geelong, who used to live on a farm at Balliang, what's your favourite dance?'

'The foxtrot.'

'May I book the foxtrot with you on that fancy card of yours?'

'Yes, you may,' says Bess, smiling.

He sees the two girls making their way back from the cloakroom and he knows at once they are Bessie's sisters. He nods his head goodbye, puts his hand on his heart and says, 'I hold my breath until the foxtrot.' Then turns on his heels and is gone.

'Who's the dish?' says Tilly with a nudge.

'He's new, isn't he?' says Honor.

'His name is Jock Connor. He's an Englishman,' said Bessie. 'And he's booked the foxtrot with me.'

'He's smooth. How did he know your favourite dance?' asked Honor.

'He asked,' said Bess, a hint of flush on her cheeks.

The band began the first set with the barn dance, followed by the waltz, then the quickstep. Jock rested against the wall under a red Chinese lantern and watched Bessie. He liked her smile and how she chatted easily with people.

The music stopped. The bandmaster walked over to the microphone in the middle of the stage and announced, 'Ladies and gentlemen, the next dance is the foxtrot.'

Jock waited and watched to see what Bess' next moves were. She looked around the room and saw he was leaning on the wall. She waved her dance card and Jock made his way over to her. 'Wasn't sure whether you were to find me or I was to find you,' he said. 'Didn't want to get this wrong.'

'The blokes usually find the girls. But, this time, you're forgiven; but only this time. Next time there will be no favours.' Bess smiled at him again.

Next time, she said next time, thought Jock and smiled too. He raised his left hand, ready to begin the dance. She took a step towards him. When the band commenced, they stepped off together.

'Why are you staring?' asked Bess.

'Me! Staring! Didn't realise, I'll watch the Chinese lanterns instead.' In an exaggerated fashion, Jock looked up at the roof, making her laugh.

'Now you're being silly.'

As they danced, Bess spoke of living in Geelong and explained she was with her sisters. Jock told her snippets of life on the ship, his work and lodgings. The music finished and they stopped in the middle of the dance floor, neither one of them wanting to be the first to let go.

'There'll be a break now,' said the bandleader. 'We'll be back in twenty minutes.'

'How about a cup of punch?' Jock asked.

'Yes let's. Come over and I'll introduce you to the crowd.'

In the middle of the supper table sat a glass bowl of red punch with floating mint leaves. Bessie introduced him to Honor, Tilly and their friend Ralph Flowers. Jock said hello to the sisters and shook Ralph's hand. 'I've seen you at the mill.'

'That's right, mate; seen you too,' replied Ralph. Ralph had red hair thinning on top and a face full of freckles. Jock noticed a gap between his front teeth and when he pronounced words with an 's' he spoke with a slight whistle.

Jock ladled punch into two cups and handed one to Bessie. 'Any more dances free on your dance card?'

'The band plays the foxtrot more than once during the evening,' she said as she sipped punch. 'And your name is next to that dance.'

The foxtrot played four times that evening.

The following Saturday night, when Jock met Bess outside the local picture theatre, the three sisters turned up together again.

'Safety in numbers, eh?'

'My father isn't partial to me going out with boys. So my sisters and I cover for one another.'

When the lights dimmed, plush red velvet curtains opened, bit by bit. Dust motes floated in a haze of blue smoke. Their arms touched. She wore a thin cardigan over her blue dress. He wore his white cotton shirt and woollen trousers.

'I'll be back in a moment,' he whispered.

Before too long he came back with a packet of Columbine caramels.

'In case we get hungry,' he said as he slipped the packet into her hand. He sat back in his seat. Their arms pressed against one another again.

'Ta, love,' she whispered into his ear.

Her breath so close startled and excited him. In time, he realised the Newsreel had been playing and became aware of men on horseback and yappy dogs herding plump woolly sheep followed by teams of men loading Australian produce onto export ships. As Jock and Bess watched women on the screen use the very latest inventions – the electric iron, gas stove, refrigerator and washing machine – a male voice over with an exaggerated faux-British accent told the audience:

The little ladies of the house are being spoilt with housework becoming easier and less time-consuming. This frees up time for entertainment and listening to the wireless. The fashions have changed, too. The little lady is now wearing light frocks with knee-length skirts and she's even cut her hair short in the flapper-style. My, my, what will we see next? And it's not just the fairer sex changing with the times. Men's pipes have been replaced by cigarettes. And clean-shaven faces have replaced beards. My word, what will become of this?

The couple sat through Charlie Chaplin's *The Little Tramp*, with neither one of them able to focus on the storyline. Bessie's presence and her perfume overwhelmed Jock. Her scent, fresh with hints of lavender and other aromas was unknown to him. Other than his sisters, he'd never been so near a girl before; it was thrilling. He was glad there was no talking allowed during the film, formulating words was a bridge too far. She'd laugh with the audience during the film, so he followed suit.

Bessie was grateful the audience found the film funny and followed their cues when to laugh. Cottonwool filled her head and the more she tried to ignore Jock's arm touching hers, the stronger her awareness. She was glad it was dark as she knew her face had flushed and hoped nervous pink blotches hadn't appeared on her neck.

When the film finished, they waited until the cinema emptied then made their way to meet Honor and Tilly. They walked along Latrobe Terrace with the two sisters in front talking and laughing. Tilly was the loudest and the most animated. As she spoke, she threw her arms around and her laugh travelled from one end of the street to the other. Honor put her hand over her sister's mouth. 'Tilly be quiet, it's late.'

Bessie and Jock dawdled behind, chatting.

'Why did you move off the farm?' Jock asked.

'It started to get too hard for Dad, and Mum too. He found work at the Ford factory on the floor. A regular income working from seven in the morning to four in the arvo is easier than life on the land.'

'Do you miss the farm?'

'I miss riding my horse. His foot went into a pothole when I was riding him a few months before we left and he broke his leg. Dad had to shoot him. It was the saddest day of my life.'

Jock looked across when he recognised the quiver in her voice.

They turned into Clarence Street and Bessie said, 'My house is just up the road. You'll have to turn back. My father will be cross if he knows I walked home with a boy.'

'Aye, are you going to the dance next Saturday?'

'I don't know. Tata now.'

Bessie caught up to her sisters and linked arms. Jock watched as the three ran together laughing and whispering, before turning into an open gate.

Jock's room at the boarding house was small, neat and comfortable. It had a single bed with a wooden bedhead, a bedside table with a porcelain jug and basin for washing, a wardrobe, chest of drawers, small writing table and a window facing the street.

He sat at the wooden table and opened his diary.

1 JUNE 1929
I've met the girl I am going to marry. Her name is Bessie Brown and she is beautiful.

He closed the book, undressed to his singlet and underpants, spread out on the bed with his hands behind his head, smiling from ear-to-ear.

This is good, he thought. This is good.

Jock filled his days with riding his bike to the mill, reading at the library, playing cricket or tennis, taking Bess to dances or the pictures. Hand in hand, they'd walk along the foreshore at Eastern Beach. Honor, Tilly and their latest beaus often joined them.

He took swimming lessons and people told him he was barmy when one day in July he stripped to his bathing trunks and went for a dip. It was a warm day – as mild as many of the summers he had known in England.

But the heady days of the 1920s were coming to an abrupt end. Australia's dependence on agricultural and industrial exports meant it was one of the countries hardest hit by America's Wall Street Crash in October 1929. Falling export demand and commodity prices placed a massive downward pressure on the economy. The woollen mills kept their doors open but were forced to cut staff. Jock kept his job but his shifts were shortened. He had just enough to live on and a few letters posted home were empty of pound notes. The basic wage was reduced by ten per cent, government funding was cut and unemployment increased.

On his way to work each day, he rode past a kiosk selling newspapers, magazines, cigarettes and sweets. He'd scan the broadsheet's headlines behind the wire frame leaning against the booth's wall. One day, a crowd had gathered in front of the kiosk hindering his view. He jumped off his bike, propped it against the lamppost and moved towards the front of the throng. In large print, the day's headline read *GREAT DEPRESSION HITS AUSTRALIA*.

Bess and Jock courted during one of the toughest times in Australia's history. By 1932, around sixty thousand women, men and children took to the road for survival. Families walked the dusty roads of rural Australia knocking on strangers' doors, begging for stale bread, a cup of soup, food scraps of any kind. One in five men had lost his job and unemployment peaked at around thirty per cent. Without work and a steady income, families lost their homes and were forced to live in makeshift dwellings of corrugated iron and hessian bags with dirt floors, inadequate heating and no sanitation. Many were forced onto the streets to stand in line at soup kitchens or beg for food.

They didn't have much but were better off than many. While living frugal lives, Jock and Bess still found ways to enjoy themselves. The group often played tennis followed by a picnic lunch on the foreshore. On one such day, the sisters had spread out a blanket under a Norfolk Island pine. Tilly was dolled up as she had invited a new boy to join them. She had wrapped a red scarf around her head and wore a checked blouse tied in a knot at her waist, white shorts and sandshoes.

'Lunch won't be long,' Tilly said. She had made jam sandwiches from a tin Mary had found at the back of the cupboard and homemade bread. Honor was laying out the plates and serviettes. Bess had picked figs from their tree and placed them in a china bowl on the tablecloth.

'Just waiting for a friend,' Tilly said, peering along the path.

Ralph and Jock sat on a bench a few yards away. 'Tilly's sweet on a new bloke,' said Ralph. 'And I'm sweet on Honor but she doesn't know I'm alive. I get so tongue-tied when I'm with her,' he said, peeling dried paint from the back of the seat. 'She's the quietest of the three and I'm not sure whether that's because she's shy or just not interested.'

'Have you asked her what she thinks of you, lad?' asked Jock.

'Crikey no, couldn't do that,' said Ralph. 'How are you and Bess getting on?'

Jock shrugged. 'Not sure. It seems good when we're together. But she hasn't invited me home to meet her parents yet. So I'm not sure whether she's as keen as me. Don't know what I should make of it.'

'Old man Brown is a bit of a tyrant – Irish,' said Ralph. 'And you know how much the Irish dislike the English.'

Jock swung around to face him. 'I am Irish! The Connors moved over from County Cork in the potato famine.'

'Does Bess know?'

Mary, Bess, Honor and Tilly squashed onto a worn couch; Frank and Jock sat on the other. Tom tuned the wireless to the station and turned up the volume. The radio was Tom's pride and joy and visitors were often ushered into the lounge room to listen. 'News will be on shortly,' he said as he stood by the mantelpiece, rocking back and forth with both hands in his pockets jingling small change.

The sound of ABC presenter Margaret Doyle's cultured tones hushed the group:

The Depression has created solidarity amongst the working class and Australians pull together in times of need. A familiar sight today is the swagman; jobless and on foot, he tries his luck in farming areas. He carries his world on his back. You usually hear him before you see him with battered saucepans and frying pans tied to his swag. If a man goes fishing, he shares his catch with his neighbours. Mothers make the most of what they have. Children have been seen walking to school barefoot in clothes made out of hessian sugar bags and underwear made from calico flour bags. It is not uncommon to see *Sydney Flour* stamped in red on small bottoms.

When the news finished, Tom switched off the wireless and left the room. One by one, the others followed, leaving Bess and Jock together. 'That wasn't too hard, was it?' Bess asked as she moved next to him. She smiled and took his hand.

Before Jock answered Tom called out from the kitchen, 'And

you better be on your way too now, Jock.'

That night Jock's diary reflected the times.

2 JULY 1932

It's been three years since I met Bess and today was the first time I met her parents. Mrs Brown is quite grand. I don't know about Mr Brown. I'd like to ask the old man for permission to marry Bess, but I'm not sure what he thinks of me. I should ask Bess first I suppose. Not sure whether she'd have me. Got nothing to offer. Worried I might lose my job at the mill. Don't know why I still have a job. Single men are the first to be sacked. I'm doing the work of two men. Operating the double lot of looms keeps me on my toes alright. Don't stop from when I first step on the floor until I clock off. Not complaining. Told the boss I'd do anything to keep the mill going. If I get marching orders I will be on the street, too. Other than the bit I have saved, I have nothing here to fall back on.

Bess hadn't seen it coming.

Jock had asked her to go for a walk by the foreshore one Sunday afternoon. On that day, he was distracted, lost in thought and not his usual chatty self. It was spring and a fresh cool breeze fanned their faces as they walked arm in arm along Eastern Beach. They veered off the path to the park. Warmer weather had brought people out from their winter hibernation. A family walked in front of the couple and a small child ran ahead of her parents holding the end of a long piece of string attached to a kite. Bess watched as the red, blue and yellow fabric dipped and rose in the sky. As they approached the rotunda, she noticed daffodils beginning to sprout at the bottom of the steps. She was put off by Jock's silence. It was new. She had only ever known him to be talkative.

Bess was pleased she had worn her coat. The sea breeze had a bite to it. Inside the shelter, out of the wind, she took off her jacket, folded it inside out and placed it on the bench, making a cushion for the pair of them to sit on in their favourite spot with a view of the trees. 'You've been very quiet today, love,' she said.

'I am, Bess. I have something on my mind. I don't know how to tell you.'

She thought the worst. He's never stuck for words. Here it comes. He wants to finish with me. I know, he's made his mind up to return to England and he doesn't know how to tell me. Why didn't he just write me a letter and let me keep my pride?

Jock first saw it by accident.

He was riding along Malop Street when he lost traction. He knew it was a puncture and moved onto the pavement to patch the inner tube. He tilted his bicycle against the window of Johnsons the Jewellers. And there it was. A thin gold band with a small chip of a diamond perched on top. He put a deposit on the ring the following week and made instalments every pay.

Jock's uncustomary silence caused Bess' chest to tighten. She wanted to run away, as she thought the worst. He began to speak when two small boys raced up the stairs into the rotunda then ran out the other side. She wanted to cry but was too proud. Why did he ask me to go for a walk just to leave me embarrassed? How will I tell everyone? No boy is going to toss me aside. She noticed sweat on his brow. If anyone does the tossing, it will be me. She took a deep breath, swallowed hard and said, 'Jock I think we should stop seeing one another.'

He stood and walked away from her, then turned. 'You think we should what?' He shook his head. 'I don't understand, why? What have I done? Are you daft? Is this what you want, really – to stop seeing one another?'

'I thought that's what you wanted,' Bess said as she dabbed at her eyes with her handkerchief. 'That's why you've been so quiet, you wanted to finish with me, or you were going back to England and you didn't know how to tell me.'

Jock knelt on one knee, took a small blue box out of his suit-coat pocket and flipped open the top lid.

Mum told me she was attracted to Dad because he was a good man. He didn't drink or gamble. I trust there was more to it than that, but she never spoke of it. I didn't ask Dad why he was attracted to Mum. It wasn't something you did in our family. My guess it was because she was beautiful, funny and warm. His diary entries show he was well and truly smitten.

There is a black-and-white photograph of Bess and Jock around the time they announced their engagement. Bess must have been twenty-six and Jock twenty-nine. They are standing side-on. Bess is in front of Jock and he has his arms around her waist. Her hands are on top of his. Her thick dark curly hair is cut in the fashionable flapper-style. She is pencil-thin and wore a calf-length linen tennis skirt, a sleeveless knitted cardigan over a plain linen shirt, socks and tennis shoes. She is leaning back on Jock. Her attention is taken by something outside of the photograph.

Jock's hair is thick, curly and black. It is cut short at the back and sides and left longer on top, causing the curls to flop either side of the middle part. He's smiling at the camera and wearing a pale shirt tucked into baggy shorts, tennis socks and shoes.

They were married on a hot, windy Saturday in February 1934. Bess borrowed a wedding dress and veil and Jock borrowed a suit. Honor and Tilly were bridesmaids. Ralph was Jock's best man and Frank his groomsman. Guests attended the church and after the ceremony, afternoon tea was served at the Brown's house. The newlyweds then caught a bus to the seaside where they booked into the Queenscliff Hotel for two nights. On their return, they rented a small one-bedroom cottage in Anne Street, not far from the Brown's family home. Without much furniture, Bess did her best by decorating it with crockery, vases, pictures, and doilies they received as wedding presents.

Jock wrote to his mother with his good news on flimsy airmail writing paper, folded it in thirds then placed the letter in a pale blue envelope with PAR AVION written in the left-hand corner. Three months later, he received a wedding card from his family. It had been sent by ship.

As the economy recovered, the country relied on exports to crawl out of the Depression, Jock's hours at the mill improved and Bess found part-time work as a housekeeper, cleaning and cooking in Mrs Roger's boarding house in south Geelong.

Bess was beginning to show when it happened. Cramps caused her to double over as she hung out washing at the boarding house. She struggled into the kitchen, sat on the nearest chair then noticed blood trickling down her legs. Mrs Rogers called for a taxi to take her to the hospital.

It was the first of three miscarriages. Bess learned to read the signs of her body and knew when the small creature inside her was slipping away from the safe harbour of her womb. With the fourth pregnancy, dread mingled with joy. Not again. She didn't visit the doctor, told no-one and tried to put it out of her mind. Within weeks her frocks strained around her middle and loose aprons no longer covered her bulge. She wanted to be happy and to tell her husband but wasn't brave enough to put a name to her pregnancy. If she spoke it out loud, something dreadful might happen. Motherhood would be out of reach again.

Jock was at cricket practice and she knew he'd be home late. In front of the mirror, she undid her dress, letting it balloon onto the ground around her. She stood in her stockinged feet and petticoat, turned side-on and rubbed her hand around her belly. She wasn't aware of Jock standing in the doorway watching her talk to their unborn child.

Mum told me this story in her later years. At one stage, she paused then smiled at me. 'Your father had said, "My God, you are gorgeous."'

Bess blossomed during pregnancy. She still carried out light duties at the boarding house: dusting, setting the table and cooking light meals. Tilly and Honor knitted matching bootees, bonnets and matinee jackets in white and cream. Mary made a patchwork quilt for the cot out of discarded clothes and Tom spruced up an old pram handed on from one of their neighbours.

Bess gave birth to a baby girl with dark hair and blue eyes. She was small and peaky. Jock named her, 'Let's call her Bridget, my mother's second name.'

Little Bridget didn't feed well from the beginning and grizzled during her waking hours. She lost weight and had dark rings under her eyes. Bess sat for hours with the baby at her breast, trying to feed her, but Bridget lost interest. It was as if she didn't have the strength to suckle. At six weeks, the infant was admitted to hospital. Bess and Jock sat in a stark waiting room with grey walls, grey linoleum and hard wooden chairs. My mother needed to feed and told the nurse her breasts were leaking and ached, and she asked if it was possible for her to nurse.

'Doctor will be out in a moment. He's examining the baby now,' was the curt response.

After waiting hours, the doctor emerged. Bess hadn't seen this man before. He was a specialist. My parents followed him along a corridor past a nursery where rows and rows of babies slept.

They were ushered into a tiny room.

'There's no easy way to say this,' the doctor said. 'Your baby has a hole in the heart and it will be a matter of days before we lose her. I am surprised she has lasted this long. It's best you both go home, try to sleep and come back in the morning. You may have a long few days ahead of you.'

Before sun-up, Bess and Jock walked arm in arm in silence back to the hospital. People were making their way to work and the warm January air was a signpost another scorcher was on its way. Jock pushed open the heavy front door of the hospital and they made their way to the room where they spent hours waiting the previous evening. It wasn't long before they were ushered through to another small room.

Bridget had died during the night. When Bess asked to see her baby, to hold her, to say goodbye, she was told Bridget's body had been dispensed with. She put her head in her hands and howled – a long primeval animal sound – then rocked back and forth crying, 'No, no, no.' Jock sat motionless, silent, staring into nothingness; both in their separate pain, unable to reach out to the other.

The next day, Jock cycled to work and went through the motions of operating the looms. He spoke to no-one. Bess stayed with her parents until Jock collected her after work. Tom and Mary had taken away the cot, pram, baby clothes and any evidence of little Bridget. The Anne Street cottage looked as it had when the couple moved in as newlyweds. Except now the joy of new marriage and beginnings had been replaced with sadness, grief and silence. Bridget's aroma lingered on their bedspread. Bess had placed her there after bath time, propped herself up on one elbow and gazed into her newborn's eyes. Her nightdress reeked of breast milk. Home alone, she found these personal relics and breathed in what was left of Bridget, buried her face in the nightgown and bedspread and cried, sobbed, howled, her tears blending with Bridget's scent. In time, the sour milk smell became too much and the nightgown was eventually laundered. Not the bedspread, though. Bess hung on as long as possible to any trace of her baby girl and would lie face down on the candlewick, breathing in Bridget's sweet baby aroma, until one day, there was no outward trace of Bridget left. The eiderdown just smelled like an eiderdown.

Bridget was rarely mentioned when I was growing up. I knew she died a few weeks after birth and shared the same birthday as me – bookend girls in a family of six children. A short time before Mum died, I asked her about the death of her firstborn. I told her the pain of losing a child was unimaginable. She cried during the telling of this story. I cried with her for myriad reasons, for the loss of the sister I didn't know, for Mum's hurt and as one mother with another.

3 September 1939

Once a week, Bess and Jock had tea at Mary and Tom's house and then afterwards Tom insisted they sit in the lounge room and listen to the wireless, whether it was the ABC News or a serial. This was the rhythm of the evening and no discussion otherwise was entered into. On this night, the Prime Minister Robert Menzies was to address the nation.

Mary had cooked corned beef with potatoes, peas and beans from the garden. The sisters washed up the dishes while Tom and Jock smoked in the lounge room. Frank had found a job cutting sugarcane in Queensland and the house appeared empty to Bess without her little brother's jokes and antics. She loved spending time with her sisters and missed their chats and giggles. Tilly had a crush on a new boy and Honor was still pondering whether she should get serious with Ralph or not. Bess had felt signs of pregnancy but kept it to herself. Tales of Tilly's latest beau and gossip from the dances were a welcomed distraction and tonic for her.

When the ABC News music wafted into the kitchen the sisters rushed into the lounge room. Bess squeezed in next to Jock just in time. Do stay tuned for an important message from the Prime Minister of Australia Robert Menzies:

My fellow Australians. It is my melancholy duty to inform you, officially, that, in the consequence of the persistence by Germany in her invasion of Poland, Great Britain has declared war upon her, and that, as a result, Australia is also at war …

'Oh no,' said Mary. 'We've lived through losing our boys in one war and now another.' As an afterthought, she said, 'I hope Frank doesn't enlist.'

'We'll be alright, won't we?' asked Tilly. 'They won't bomb us, will they?'

'Of course not, you stupid girl,' said Tom. 'Germany's at war with England, not Australia.' Tom stood up and switched off the wireless. 'Pig-iron Bob has no right to dump us into someone else's war.'

Jock looked up at him. 'My brothers will join up, there is no doubt, and maybe my sisters too, to nurse the wounded.' All eyes turned to him as the realisation of what war meant sank in.

Bess held Jock's hand then turned her attention to her father. She had never stood up to Tom before, but that night she had no fear. 'That someone else's war is my husband's and your son-in-law's family.'

Tom coloured, ran his fingers through his hair, walked over to where Jock was sitting and put his hand on his shoulder. 'Sorry, son, I don't think of you as anyone else but one of us.' His uncustomary regard for Jock didn't go unnoticed and the women in the room exchanged glances.

Jock was torn as to where his responsibilities lay. He knew he had to join up; but how to tell Bess? She had dealt with enough with little Bridget's death. He saw the pain on her face when her gaze lingered on babies in prams and mothers' arms. At the thought of Bridget, tears welled in his eyes. He blinked hard and swallowed. How will she cope now losing her husband to the army?

AUSTRALIA AT WAR! loomed the headline from the wire rack on his ride to work; posters had been stuck to lampposts along La Trobe Terrace urging men to enlist. 'They didn't waste much time,' Jock said to himself. His thoughts raced. My brothers and lads I know back home will be joining up to fight and I'm on the other side of the world married with a good job and a second family. My first priority is Bess, but I know I should fight for England.

He rode to the mill and slipped his front wheel into the bike stand. War-talk was rife as he made his way to the weaving room. He was thankful for the noise from the looms. It offered him time to think and work out what he should do.

Bess' pregnancy was confirmed a few weeks after the Prime Minister's announcement. Jock was thrilled with the news, but more undecided as to enlist or not. He had received letters from home telling him his two younger brothers were fighting in France. Much to Mary's grief, Frank had enlisted and was in the first shipment of men sent to Mount Martha for training. Ralph had joined up too.

On Christmas Eve, Tom collapsed while working in his shed. Mary found him on the floor behind a stack of wooden boxes. He died hours later from a massive heart attack. The funeral took place the following week at the same church Jock and Bess had been married in six years earlier. A large congregation attended and Jock was one of the six pallbearers who carried Tom's coffin. With the weight of the wooden box on his shoulders, his thoughts went to the time when his father died. He had been too young to carry him from the church but remembered walking behind the pallbearers that day and hearing his mother next to him crying as they made their way out of the church into the icy wind.

Tom was buried in the Geelong Eastern Cemetery. The fact that no representative from Tom's side attended was not lost on Jock. It made him even more mindful of his family back in England, with thoughts of them at war never far away.

Sadness hung over the Clarence Street house and Mary stayed in bed most days. Honor and Tilly took turns in taking their mother meals and they'd try to coax her to help with a patchwork quilt or join them for a walk along the foreshore. Bess visited daily and one morning sat on her mother's bed and placed Mary's hand on her stomach as the baby kicked.

'Feel this, Mum,' she said.

It was in the evenings when Honor and Tilly missed their father the most. Mary had banned the radio. It had become impossible for her to separate hearing the wireless from Tom. For her, the two were entwined.

Jock had taken on the man of the house role and helped out where required. He'd trim the high branches in the trees, clean out the gutters or shift any heavy items Mary needed moved. As the months passed, she gained weight and cooked for her family again. In time, the sound of the wireless floated through the house as the women tried to get on with life without the towering presence of Tom Brown.

It was four in the morning when Bess shook Jock by the shoulder. 'It's time.'

He ran to the telephone box on the corner and phoned for a taxi. By the time he returned, Bess was on her hands and knees panting. 'Get Mum, the baby's coming.'

Mary delivered her first grandson on the kitchen floor of Jock and Bess' cottage. Cleary Thomas Connor weighed eight pounds, three ounces. The midwife visited the next day and gave the 'all clear' to the baby boy.

As the weeks passed, Cleary fed and slept well. He put on weight and Bess grew more in love with him every day. Her mother and sisters visited with pots of soup, baked cakes and knitted baby clothes. On their walks with little Cleary sleeping in the pram, Jock noticed the lack of civilian men in the streets. Factories were now beginning to hire women.

Jock stood in the doorway taking in the sweet domestic scene in front of him. Bess stood barefoot on the linoleum, stirring a pot on the stove singing to Cleary lying on a blanket in a sunny patch on the floor. She turned.

'Hello, love. What's up, you look as if your dog's died?'

'I've joined up,' Jock said. 'Leave Wednesday.' He made an attempt to smile.

Bess felt she was supposed to reciprocate with goodwill but didn't know how. She picked Cleary up from the floor. Afternoon sun threw golden lights on his baby curls and he chuckled as he was lifted into the air. She placed him in the wooden highchair, mixed boiled potato and pumpkin in a chipped white enamel mug and plopped a teaspoon of butter into the mash.

'Just be eighteen months pet, no longer than that,' he said. 'There'll be regular money.'

'You've got regular money at the mill, now.'

Bess mixed the vegetables in a gentle rhythm at first, but the more Jock talked of leaving, the escapades ahead of him and catching up with Frank and Ralph, the harder and faster she stirred. The sound of the fork clinked against the enamel mug. Jock walked over to his wife, slipped his arm around her waist and tried to make a joke of it.

'Pet, you're mixing the baby's food not ringing a chook's neck.'
Bess was silent.

'Well, maybe twelve months, love.'

'This is out of the blue, how long had you been thinking of this?'

'Since Menzies' announcement last year.'

'Last year!' She spun around to look at him. 'You didn't mention it – I didn't know you were thinking of enlisting.'

'I know, pet. There didn't appear to be the right time; you were pregnant, Tom died, then Cleary was born. And it's something a man has to think about on his own.'

'Oh is that right? So I don't have a say. Is that what you're saying?'

'I didn't mean that, love.' Jock walked over to the kitchen window, looked out onto the back garden. He thought of England and his brothers fighting. He moved to where Bess was standing and took the enamel mug and placed it on the table. He held her hands. 'It's just, well … it's England that's at war, Bess – my country. It will be alright love, I promise. I'll be back before you know, pet.'

She was left with the aroma of Craven As mixed and the smell of his woollen army coat. She held Cleary on her left hip as she waved and did her best to smile. Bess hugged her son tighter and feared for her husband's safety. She missed him even as she watched him walk up Anne Street towards the Geelong Railway Station.

'I'll write, pet,' he said, walking backwards along the footpath. 'I'll write.'

THE WAR

July 1941

THE GHAN SNAKED NORTH through the central Australian desert on its way to Alice Springs, the end of the line. Soldiers squeezed in anywhere possible, on the floor, even in the luggage racks. Jock had managed a window seat.

Talk of enemy reconnaissance planes flying at night meant the train stopped at dusk. The Ghan pulled up in what appeared to Jock the middle of nowhere. When he jumped to the ground, a cloud of red dust covered his army boots and socks. It was a relief to stretch his legs after being cramped for so long. He walked to the front of the train and rolled off large tin drums from the open-topped carriages. Sticks Malone and Stan Stainsbury searched for fuel – dried twigs and dead bushes.

At sundown, men donned their greatcoats and huddled around fires lit low in rusty bins. Punctured drum lids hindered the warm glow being seen from the air. Jock rubbed his hands together and held them splayed over the heat. He pulled a cigarette from his coat pocket and placed it in his mouth.

Stan lit his own rollie then Jock's, before throwing the match into the flames.

'Third time unlucky. My old man used to say that. First strike the Turks see you. Second light they take aim. Third light, boom you're dead.' Stan sucked hard on his cigarette.

Sounds of the night enveloped them, the crackling fire, movement from animals in the bush and in the distance Aborigines singing accompanied by the clack-clack of their bilma.

'Never thought I'd miss Ballarat,' said Stan. Tall and muscular with a thin face, high cheekbones and receding hairline, Leonard 'Stan' Stainsbury threw his head back when he laughed. His smile crooked, adapted to hide a couple of missing teeth.

'Been wanting to get away from my old man for years,' Stan said as he stared at the drum. 'Always picking on me he was. Telling me I was bone idle and useless.' He pulled the lapels of his coat up around his ears to keep out the night chill.

'Hated Ballarat, hated school; left school two days after I turned twelve.' He drew on his cigarette, tilted his face towards the billion stars and blew smoke into the night air.

'Helped Mum full-time then, packing and delivering the groceries on my bike. The old man got mad after a few bottles and lashed out at Mum for nothing. He'd make stuff up that she had or hadn't done, so I'd stand in between them. "Hit me, you bludger," I'd say. He did, plenty of times; that's how I lost these two teeth.' He lifted his top gum to expose the gap. 'Until I got to sixteen and grew a good few inches in that year. He moved from me to my little sisters, Dulcie and Betty – couldn't stand it. So I took to him with a pick handle. He skedaddled out of town and we haven't seen him since.'

'Remind me never to upset you then, mate,' said Jock. 'I'm not too partial to pick handles, myself.'

The men laughed in unison then stood in silence staring at the flames, a couple kicked the dirt.

'My mum cried when I enlisted,' said Stan.

'So did mine,' said Horry.

'And mine,' said Sticks Malone.

Jock remained silent with that familiar tightness in the pit of his stomach as he remembered his mother rolling over and pulling the blanket over her head the day he left England.

In the distance, Aborigines chanted. The men listened in silence to the soulful sound drifting through the darkness.

'She told me, don't end up like your father,' Stan continued. 'Mum reckoned the old man came back from the war different. Reckoned he didn't drink and wasn't violent before he left for Turkey. But ever since I can remember he always had a bottle or glass in his hand and she was often bruised or had a cut lip.'

The fire began to subside. Jock threw more sticks into the drum and kicked the rusty sides a couple of times to stir the embers. The smoke smelled of eucalyptus.

'It was so different after he left, so good. After tea, we'd play cards – Mum, me, Dulcie and Betty together at the kitchen table with the wireless on, never frightened of the back screen door opening as before. I knew it'd be alright – me leaving – 'cause I found out the old man had died in a blue in Melbourne during an Anzac Day two-up game. Not sure whether Mum knew. I didn't tell her. But I knew they'd be alright.'

Stan stared into the fire. They all did.

The clacking of the bilmas in the distance started up again.

'Now look at me, out in the middle of Woop Woop on the way to Darwin with a pack of miserable bastards. Who'd have thought?'

Sticks Malone put his clenched fist to his mouth and cleared his throat. 'My mum cried for a day. She went upstairs to her bedroom and when she came back down, she just stopped talking to me. She just went quiet. Her brother, my Uncle Harry, didn't return from Flanders. I think it had something to do with that.'

Sticks stood at six foot four with long skinny legs. The army barbers lost the fight against his curly blonde hair. It sat in waves on top of his head and as it grew, corkscrew curls popped up. He was from New South Wales, the first son of a wealthy grazier. Educated at boarding school in Sydney, he was expected to go to university then take over the property from his father.

'I thought enlisting would be a good chance to see the world for a couple of years before settling down. It's not that I don't want to be on the land, I do, just not now.'

What a leveller the war is, Jock thought. Here is a lad who left school at twelve and ran his father out of town with a pick handle, and another wealthy, well-educated lad, who went to boarding school, and me, standing around the same fire.

'What do they call you at home, Sticks?' Jock asked.

'I was christened Miriam William Malone after my great-grandfather.'

Glad it was pitch-dark, Sticks felt his face burning with embarrassment.

'I hate the name Miriam, usually tell people my name's Will.'

'You're Sticks to us, mate,' said a voice from the back of the huddle.

My mother told me the letters she received from Dad while he was stationed in Darwin had been censored with sections sliced out with a razor blade. I found a letter folded in four and tucked in the back of one of his diaries. It was written on a torn-out page from one of his journals. The writing had faded with age and it took me a while to decipher his script. It had been written in lead pencil.

OCTOBER 1941

My dear Bess,

It seems ages since I left No. 43 and I miss you and the baby dreadfully. We're stationed in Darwin and it's the last frontier up here. I've never seen such rain, pet – 72 hours without let-up last week and the army rations us with one bottle of water a day. It doesn't make sense. A lot of what the army does doesn't make sense. The locals said the wet season started early. We were told it doesn't usually come until later in the year. The mud and slush make getting around difficult. I'm stationed at Winnellie Barracks and we have been underwater. We've been given camp stretchers left over from the First World War. They're mouldy and worn. But it beats sleeping on the wet floor. We're building roads and erecting telegraph poles. Hard work in the heat. Not much to report, just that it's as hot as blazes and it's not even summer yet. I've never imagined such heat and humidity.

We arrived in Darwin weeks ago. It is hard to keep track. We've been sent here to acclimatise to the tropics before heading further north to New Guinea. We only had 24 hours' notice to leave Pucka. Then it was full steam ahead. The Japs are well and truly entrenched in the NG jungles and we're to relieve blokes in the 9th Division who haven't had a break in ages. Have no idea when we are to ship out, though. Next letter from me may be from the jungles of NG. Who knows?

The trip up through central Australia was a marvel. We left Pucka and caught the train at Seymour, which took us to Melbourne and then overnight to Adelaide. Then onto the Ghan to Alice Springs. We stopped at Murray Bridge and Quorn where the girls from the CWA were waiting for us with hot tea, freshly cut sandwiches and Anzac biscuits. It tasted good, manna from heaven after the slush served at Pucka. When the train moved out of the station, the girls stayed on the platform waving their hankies and singing 'Waltzing Matilda'. I watched them until they became so small they were hard to make out. All I could think of was you.

Bess, the Australian countryside is indescribable. It's like being on another planet. Wild camels roam in packs. They are the ugliest and dirtiest creatures I've ever seen. And dangerous too. Apparently, they kick and spit if you get too close. The ground was so dry, as if it's never seen rain. Hot, dusty and dry. The further north we travelled the hotter it got. The days were roasting so we'd strip to our singlets and shorts. Then at night the temperature dropped.

The train stopped and on went the big coats, as it got chilly. We'd stand around fires lit in big tin drums trying to keep warm. The train didn't move at night because of the blackout. It's a risk having the lights on. There's been talk of Jap reconnaissance planes.

The blokes said it was freezing, but no disrespect to them, they don't know what freezing is. We'd have a sing-a-long some nights and I played the spoons and Snowy White, a fella from Coober Pedy, played the mouth organ. There were songs I didn't know, but I am getting to know them. Sometimes we'd tell stories. I'm with a great mob of blokes, Bess. We have plenty of laughs and I give as good as I get. The most well-used line is that they need an interpreter to help them understand what I am saying, especially when I get excited and my speech quickens. I can fall back into dialect and then I am left with a group of lads looking at me with big grins on their faces. It's good fun.

The night sky through the middle of Australia was the blackest of black with a million stars that went on forever. I've never seen anything like it, love. In snuffy Manchester, smog and fog blanketed the stars. But travelling up through the middle, the air was so pure, crisp and clean. It's a wonder, Bess. The sunsets and sunrises were magnificent – spectacular – crimson, orange and gold. And so much land, as far as your eye can see, not a house, not a person, except for a few Aborigines. I wish you could see what I see, love. It saddens me that you can't. We'll see Australia together one day, I promise.

I saw my first mob of Aborigines, third day in. What a sight! They were lean and nearly naked except for pieces of well-placed cloth and they walked in groups. The men had spears and one had a dead kangaroo slumped over his shoulder. The women, gins they call them, and their children walked together away from the men and they scanned the ground as if they'd lost something. Then they'd stop and pick something from dead bushes. Well, that's what it looked like to me. They'd place their takings into oval-shaped wooden dishes carried on their heads. I was taken by their grace and ease as they step light upon the ground. I was mesmerised by them. The other blokes call them abos, darkies and boongs. They were cruel in what they were saying. Not to be repeated. But it's so new to me, pet. I left Lancashire over a decade ago and now I am seeing and experiencing things I never dreamed of.

The train stopped at Alice Springs as that's the end of the tracks. Then we were driven to Darwin along unmade corrugated roads. It was the most dreadful ride. Every bone in my body shook.

Not much to tell you about what's going on up here. Just that it's hot as blazes. I'll write later, love, as the mailbag is due and I don't want to miss this post as I can't be sure of the next delivery. There is no rhyme nor reason to it. Typical army.

Give my regards to your mother, Honor and Tilly. A big kiss to you and the baby.

Any news from Frank and Ralph? I lost touch after Puckapunyal. God bless.

Love Jock

Their task was to set up a WS FS6 MK II Wireless in the scrub between Darwin and Adelaide River. Sticks jumped in the driver's seat. Jock and Stan climbed into the truck's open-tray. Jock stamped his boot hard on a hessian bag filled with tools to stop it sliding. The vehicle took off in a cloud of red dust and headed inland, racing over low-lying scrub, through and over potholes. It wasn't long before they came to thick bush with miles of gum and cypress trees.

Jock dragged the two-man saw from the hessian bag and handed one end to Stan. The teeth of the saw were rusted and worn making cutting the trees slow and arduous. Stripped to the waist, they tried to find trees in shaded patches to gain relief from the scorching sun. Flies stuck to their faces, backs, nostrils. It took most of the day to cut enough trees to fill the truck.

Jock noticed thick dark clouds rolling in from the ocean, which took the sting out of the sun but added another risk. Sticks saw the clouds too. 'We need to get back to base before the storm breaks. It's dangerous out here with lightning.'

'Especially under these trees, we're asking for trouble,' said Stan as he pulled the rope tight across the load and secured it tight.

The next day Jock was in the bush again working along the 600-mile stretch from Darwin to Tennant Creek. Bulldozers and small loaders made light work of the construction. Surveyors pegged the route then bulldozer crews cleared sections of the track six and a half yards wide followed by teams measuring out the distance between the poles and placing a marker where each hole was to be dug. Diggers equipped with augers, jackhammers and explosives followed. Materials required for each pole site were dropped close by then assembled to fit on each cross-arm. A pole was lowered into the hole where it leaned until the next group came to set it upright, drop in the backfill and attach the stays. When each section of poles was erected, the line parties went into action reeling out six pairs of wire simultaneously. Men followed with hook sticks to lift it over the cross-arms to wait for linesmen to tighten the wires at each pole. Lines were tied to poles by cable or rope.

It took two men to haul the radio's grey cumbersome metal casing from the truck to a well-treed place hidden from enemy planes. Confident of its position, they walked back to the vehicle, picked up a large battery and set it next to the radio. Jock threw a wire high into a gum tree to act as an aerial, then sat on a rock, took out the recording sheet and HB pencil. He hung his hat on a branch of a broken tree he used as a backrest, swiped the flies on his back, arms and face with a strip of gum tree leaves and placed the earphones over both ears.

The wireless had knobs and dials across the top two-thirds of one side. At the bottom left-hand side was a black round knob, attached to a thin piece of metal that moved up and down. Jock twiddled the knobs and dials looking for the right wavelength. When satisfied, he placed his right hand on the black round knob and leaned closer to the set. He turned his head to one side as if communing with the metal square case in front of him. His hand movements were soft and gentle as he tapped out a series of sounds – dit, dit, dah, dah.

'I'll be buggered if I can figure out what that tap, tap, tapping means,' said Stan.

'Quiet,' Sticks said.

When Jock finished, he eased his back against the tree branch and took off the earphones. Stan and Sticks stood around Jock with their hands on their hips, watching the wireless set. Within seconds, the Morse code lever started moving on its own, a return message from Winnellie Barracks. They threw their hats in the air.

'You little beauty,' Sticks said.

'Success first time,' said Stan.

'Ay,' said Jock, grinning from ear-to-ear.

Jock replaced his earphones then tried the two speech circuits. The voices at the other end were faint but audible.

19 February 1942

The day started out no different to every other day – hot and humid. Jock woke at six and jumped on the communal bike Tic had won from Yanks in a poker game a few weeks earlier.

The ride from Winnellie Barracks to the billabong took twenty minutes along a bumpy dirt track by the railway line. Jock stood full height on the pedals, his piston legs pushing hard, his back bent over the handlebars. Each morning he raced his time from the previous day. The faster he rode, the emptier his mind became. No thoughts, just trickles of sweat on his back, legs and arms; eyes stinging from riding head-on into the hot air. Over hills and around bends he rode, dodging holes in the road and swerving rocks. He was nearly at his destination when his calves, thighs and buttocks burned, a vice-like grip seized his chest. He had to give in. He was spent. The place of surrender that day was further than the day before, just three hundred yards from the swimming hole. Not bad, he thought, getting better. He slumped onto the worn leather bicycle seat and cruised the last bit, breathing hard, his legs dangling either side of the pedals. It was downhill and little effort was needed.

He was grateful for the use of the bike and wished he'd been there to witness the card game.

People Jock had met since leaving Melbourne seven months earlier intrigued him. Especially Tic, whose bike he was riding. His parents owned a pub in Adelaide and he had been playing cards with the regulars since he was eight. He stumbled across a card game with a bunch of Yank sailors in the back room of The Don. The Americans had had a skinful. Tic, being a publican's son, didn't touch the stuff.

'Mind if I sit in on a hand or two?'

'Sure, buddy. Have you played five-card poker before?'

'A bit.'

The Yanks' bravado increased with every hand. Except for the twitch, Tic's face didn't move. His practice was to lose the first five hands until he was skint. On the sixth, Tic began to play his game and soon after cleaned up the Yanks and walked away with thirty-five pounds plus the two-wheeler.

Jock stopped at the billabong where soldiers bathed and washed their clothes. He propped the bike against a tree stump in the morning shade, took off his shorts and y-fronts, kicked off his boots, tied the laces together and looped them over a low-lying branch. He'd learned to do that after what had happened to Horry Anderson.

Jock had taken a shine to the sixteen-year-old. He enjoyed Horry's joy for life and naivety. A big fella, already shaving, he'd told the recruitment officer in Adelaide he was eighteen. It had been Boxing Day 1941, and Horry had wanted to be first in. He dropped his shorts and threw his boots onto a pile of rocks, dive-bombed off an over-hanging tree. After his swim, the boy sat on the rocks and pulled on his boots. He tied the laces in a double knot as his mother had shown him.

'Fuck, fuck, fuckity fuck.'

Horry jumped from one foot to the other kicking at an imaginary object. He dropped on his haunches, his hands trying to undo the laces. He threw both boots into the water and kicked and brushed the biting insects off his feet. The shoes floated for a while, then filled with water and disappeared below the surface. Still dressed, he lunged in to retrieve them and emptied his waterlogged boots as he waded out of the billabong. He slipped his stinging feet into the damp leather. The bites lasted for weeks, before becoming septic in the tropical air.

The water was mirror-still. Jock took a few steps in, then duck-dived, luxuriating in the cool swoosh over his hot, sweaty body. He swam on his own for a time, rolled on his back floating and gazing at the cloudless, blue sky, forgetting where he was for a moment. His thoughts were of Bess and swimming with her at Eastern Beach before the baby came along. Jock remembered her in the blue swimsuit, the one that matched her blue-grey eyes – those eyes, those mesmerising eyes. She had worn white shorts over halter-neck bathers and slid them over her legs and feet, leaving them concertinaed on the sand. Still wearing a wide-brimmed straw hat, she tiptoed into the shoal. Not being able to swim, she was nervous around water. In time, she became more confident and paddled near the sandbars. Jock swam out further and rode the waves to where she splashed. They moved together in the shallows. Just their heads were visible above the water as the couple gazed into one another's eyes. Beneath the surface, their arms and legs were entwined.

Noise from the other blokes talking and diving into the water jarred him back into present time. The early morning dip, a welcome relief from the monstrous heat, had become a morning ritual for a group of them. The soldiers fooled around, telling the same jokes and playing the same tricks they had the day before, and the day before that.

'Hey Horry, did you leave your boots on the rocks over there mate?'

'Yeah mate, they'd be safe as houses – bull ant houses.'

At thirty-six, Jock was one of the oldest. 'Even I know to watch out for bull ants, Horry, and I'm one of those no good poms you keep bunging on about.'

Horry didn't miss a beat. 'Hey, old-timer, when I need fatherly advice I'll ask for it. Be careful you don't get your wheelchair bogged in the mud.'

No thought of war at this waterhole, thought Jock, as he swam towards Horry and splashed him. Tic snuck ashore and picked up Snowy Mac's y-fronts and threw them at their owner. Thwack! They hit Snowy right in the face. He peeled them off and threw them at one of the other swimmers. Tic picked up abandoned clothes from the bank of the billabong and the surrounding tree branches and threw them randomly at anyone in the water. The chiacking continued with muddy clothes flying back and forth.

With the best part of the day behind him and knowing he had to be picked up in less than an hour, Jock waded out of the water still smiling at the predictable lame gags. He rescued his clothes from Tic's grasp, rinsed the mud out of them and before he was dressed and on the bike, was covered in sweat again. He rode back to Winnellie, ate the usual biscuit and bully beef breakfast with weak black tea. With some time to spare before pick-up, he found a quiet place outside, sat under a gum tree, pulled out his notebook and wrote:

Singapore surrendered to Japs on the 15th. Singapore – last stop before Aust. We're sitting ducks up here. Nothing between us and Japs run south. No radars in town. Artillery scarce, less than 20 AA guns and a small number of Lewis Guns. We're supposed to be gunners but had no training since Pucka because of ammo shortages. Regiments issued with five rounds of bullets per rifle – machine-gunners, 30,000 rounds per machine-gun, which at a stretch would last five minutes. People are getting nervy. I am too. A lot of our lads were sent to defend Singapore, so the Japs couldn't attack Australia. Poor bastards are probably dead now or taken prisoner. Wonder when we will be shipped to New Guinea. Been here long enough to acclimatise to tropics. Lads sent overseas to fight for England and America taken all new artillery. Up in stinking heat of Darwin have leftover artillery from WWI. Artillery unpacked the other day was marked *not to be used in tropics*. Roadwork again today. I signed up because I'm an Englishman and wanted to fight for my old country and new one too. Not build bloody roads in the hot sun.

When not rostered on signals' duty, Jock was part of a team working on the Alice Springs to Darwin road. Bare-chested soldiers blistered and burned from the searing heat, made roads and laid railway sleepers, building a network of bases, central to the defence of Darwin. It was hot back-breaking work. Furnace-like conditions made it difficult to move fast. Jock was in a team of fifteen men. Their job was to break-up rocks on the goat track. They worked in the blazing sun. The rust-coloured dirt settled in the corners of their eyes, made its way up their noses, seeped into singlets and shorts and the pores of their skin. Dirt and sweat ran down their bodies. Mosquito bites and flies were constant. Battered tin water bottles hung from soldiers' belts. Dehydration was the enemy. One bottle of water per day was the ration. Jock wasn't sure why water was limited as there was no shortage with the wet season lasting six months. Another ridiculous army order.

The blisters on Jock's hands had healed and hardened. The pick he was given was a blunt cast-off from the First World War. He rested the smooth handle on his bony shoulder, considering the large rock before him. Hitting its centre would be the trick. He swung the pick, up and then down again with all his might. When the tip hit the rock, it bounced off and pain reverberated in every joint in his body. He was glad Horry was further along the road and didn't witness his feeble attempt. The big boulders he left for the stronger men in the team. He had more success with the smaller ones. After the rocks had been broken, they were thrown to the side of the road. Then a group followed, flattening the surface. A tar truck trailed behind spilling boiling bitumen over the roads. The stench from the black goo hung in the air.

During their morning smoko, Jock and the crew found shade under large trees with roots hanging from the branches. Brown leaves crumbled under heavy army supply boots. The sound of planes came from the south-west. Stan looked to the sky, using his hand to shield his eyes from the sun's glare.

'American Kittyhawks?'

'About bloody time,' said Snowy and leaned back on a tree stump drawing on his cigarette.

At first, Jock was reminded of penny-bungers, until he saw small explosions of dirt and shattered leaves and branches along the road they'd just cleared. Dense droning from engines increased and Jock noticed they were different from the Australian and American aircraft. Huge formations of planes, silver planes with red dots on their sides blackened the sky.

'Shit! They're the Japanese!' he said, almost to himself. Then yelled it louder. 'IT'S THE JAPS!'

Jock's ears ached from the sound of the bombing and strafing. The thunderous noise made it hard for him to think with any clarity. It was hard to work out from what direction the planes were coming. It seemed as if they were shooting from the north and the south, from the east and the west. He saw men jump into open trucks and he joined them. Yabby Young flew into the driver's seat and headed towards the wharf. They were two vehicles short because earlier in the morning, two trucks had headed back to Larrimah Barracks to pick up extra men. The soldiers piled in close together like sheep to the slaughter. Sweaty arms and legs entangled. The corrugated road made the ride hellish. Yabby drove at break-neck speed causing bodies to bounce around.

'Fuckin' hell Yabby, if the Japs don't kill us you will,' yelled Stan.

Jock landed heavily on the metal tray again and again, his bony elbows, knees and shoulders taking the full force of the impact. His body ached and all he thought of was that he didn't want to die. Not now, don't let me die now. My wife and son need me. I want to see my boy grow up. His ears rang with the sound of bombs and strafing. Explosions reverberated through the truck and his body and the sky darkened even more. The trucks sped along the foot of Stokes Hill.

As the harbour came into sight, debris covered the road causing the convoy to reduce speed. Men began yelling and jumping off the moving vehicles, some rolling then crawling for cover under bushes, behind fences or stone walls. Jock rushed towards the wharf where the explosives carrier the MV *Neptuna* was on fire and engulfed in black mushroom clouds. He watched bombs drop onto the carrier. The explosions rocked the ground, and he was thrown backwards. Those on board the *Neptuna* jumped into the burning water, black with oil; many were on fire. The scorched men's screams pierced somewhere deep inside him. Strafing along the water's edge picked off anyone trying to run for cover. Jock scrambled into the nearest slit trench, curled into a ball, put his hands over his head and attempted to say the Rosary. He could only remember *Hail Mary full of grace* ... and he repeated those five words in his head over and over. A 500-pound bomb dropped close by, then another and another, causing him to rattle around like a cork in an empty bottle. He thrashed against the sides of the trench, his shoulders and hips taking the full force. He tried to stay still, but with every explosion, he was thrown against the hard rock wall of the ditch and pummelled from head to foot. He didn't know how long it was before he realised hell had subsided.

He uncurled his hands, crept out of the slit trench and looked around for anyone he knew. He saw Tic, Snowy and men from the trucks crawl out of trenches and from behind walls. Nobody spoke; there was nothing to say; they were dazed, dirty, wounded and bruised; clothes were black and torn. Jock moved towards the harbour, drawn to the carnage, wanting, needing, to help, but not knowing what to do. The stink of burning flesh, gunpowder and faeces where men had shat themselves from the sheer horror of it, hung in the air. Salty tears – he realised he must have wept during the attack, but had no idea when. He saw charred body parts torched by the burning oil slicks bash against what was left of the wharf. Men screamed and cried out. Crew members crowded onto what was left of the USS *Peary*. The midship and stern had been bombed; sailors saluted as the ship with them on it disappeared below the surface of the choppy slate Arafura. He looked around and saw Darwin ablaze; black clouds and smoke made it difficult to see. In time, people found their voices.

'Help over here. I need help over here,' yelled Yabby, who was kneeling by a young boy covered in blood.

'On my way mate, coming,' Jock replied. Together they carried the youngster and placed him on the back of the truck, now filling with the wounded and dead.

'You'll be right there son, someone will take you to the hospital.'
'Where's my Dad? We were fishing off the pier,' the boy asked.
'He'll be right,' answered Jock. Not knowing what else to say.

Jock, Tic and Horry waded chest-deep into the sea, sometimes swimming to retrieve body parts and corpses. Burning oil caused skin to peel. Black and pink flesh hung as if thin paper. Jock and Tic swam together towards two sailors hanging on floating debris.

'I'll get this one, you get the other,' said Jock.

Tic swam further out to a sailor draped over a piece of wood. 'Gidday mate,' he said as he swam up beside him. 'Stick with me, I'll get you back.' He placed his arm under the sailor's chin, ready to swim sidestroke back to shore. The man's eyes were closed and as his head lolled back onto Tic's shoulder, he recognised the man as one of the sailors in the poker game when he won the bike.

Jock waited in thigh-deep water ready to help Tic lift the sailor onto the truck before swimming out to salvage more bodies. Jock was covered in greasy black streaks, and blisters from swimming too near the burning oil were beginning to form. Salt and oil filled his mouth. He tried to spit but had no saliva.

Tears streamed down Tic's face. Jock saw the bottom half of the man in his friend's headlock had been blown away. As they pulled his remains ashore, soldiers lifted the half-man onto the back of a truck before it sped away.

Again, the sound of the crump, crump, crump, of Mitsubishi engines – enemy planes. Strafing along the water and shore forced Jock to shelter under what was left of the pier. He lost Tic and Horry for the second time. This time, the Japanese focused on the town, leaving the harbour to burn, the boats and jetty to sink. The bombers were swift and efficient. They aimed at the Royal Australian Air Force Base and the communications centre, flying systematically along the streets, bombing everything in their wake.

In another part of town, strafing along the Esplanade caused people to scramble down dangerous cliffs to safer pockets. Three guns at a time began shooting at the enemy. Antiquated fuses marked *not to be used in tropical weather* caused the ammunition to go under and over the planes. Deafening bombs shook the ground. People yelled, ran and dived into any nook or shelter, slit trenches, gutters, under cliffs. Mushroom clouds from the harbour darkened the sky. Another bomb dropped, a man alone and on fire ran screaming, another bomb fell and another. People were ripped apart, arms and legs flung into trees. Soldiers were shooting, yelling, screaming. Hundreds of overhead silver planes dropped parcels of evil and destruction. Aircraft so low the smiling faces of the Japanese pilots were seen. The face of a child's doll was smashed, debris was everywhere. The Royal Australian Air Force Base, town centre – nowhere and no-one was spared. Thirteen warships were sunk. Wharfies were killed and ninety-one sailors died, many not yet twenty.

When the planes faded into the distance, Jock crept out and looked for his mates – anyone. He made his way into town. Black smoke hid the sun. Chaos and panic everywhere; men lay dead in trenches as if they were sleeping, still holding guns as they tried to protect the town.

He walked through twisted, tangled metal, broken concrete, shattered glass, the dead and wounded, and broken china and furniture. Skeletons of buildings stood where once a town thrived. Footpaths and roads were strewn with mangled corrugated iron, bricks and metal. Jock found it hard to work out where he was. The place was flattened and carpeted with rubble. He helped, most people did, trying to put out fires, but with limited resources, no leadership or direction – it was a matter of moving wreckage from one pile to another.

Amidst the carnage, he realised he was near the post office, telephone exchange and the cable office. A car on its roof, crushed and crumbled, had ended up where the post office counter used to be. He remembered his conversation with the Postmaster, Hurtle

Bald, on the day he posted Bess and Cleary's Christmas parcel.

'Except for a direct hit, this bomb shelter is the safest place to be in an air raid,' Bald had said.

On that day, Jock watched the ground being excavated five feet deep, thirteen feet long and three feet wide. Two railway irons running its full length were dropped in to reinforce the sandbags. A galvanised iron lid had covered the slit trench.

As Jock walked among the ruins, he was amazed at the enemy's accurate aim. A 500-pound bomb had landed right on top of the shelter, killing the nine employees of the civilian communications' base. Battered, bleeding and covered with dirt, Hurtle Bald was in a sitting position on the ground. His arms and legs looked broken. Iris, Hurtle's eighteen-year-old daughter, lay a distance from the crater with part of her head blown away. Jock remembered overhearing Iris making plans to see her friends at the Star Theatre the following Saturday night. Further on lay Emily Young, who had stayed in Darwin because she didn't want to leave her husband Jim, who owned a garage in Smith Street. Emily's head was caved in. The man hanging in the fork of a tree was unrecognisable.

Rescuers at the scene pulled the curtains from the post office windows and Jock helped cover the women's bodies until they were placed on stretchers and driven to the mortuary.

It took forty-two minutes for Darwin to be broken.

As Jock had floated on his own in the billabong that morning, dreaming of happier times with Bess and joking with his mates, four Japanese fighter ships dropped anchor two hundred and thirty-six miles off the coast. Zeros, Vals and Kates hovered over flight decks; engines roared – deafening. Propellers turned gradually at first, rotating at full speed within seconds. One by one, they took off, wheels folded. The morning sun gleamed on shiny wings. They gathered into formations and headed for their targets with their

Commander Captain Mitsuo Fuchida's orders ringing in their ears, 'Kill anything that moves.'

At 9.30 am, Father John McGrath, a missionary on Melville Island, phoned the Darwin Wireless Station alerting them to a large number of planes passing over, heading south. Lou Curnock, officer-in-charge, took the call then phoned the Royal Australian Air Force Base to relay Father McGrath's message.

'A large number of planes, high in the sky, just passed over Melville Island.'

'Don't worry. We are expecting Catalina's from Timor,' said a scratchy voice on the other end of the phone.

'How many are you expecting?'

'Half-a-dozen.'

'Well, a large number isn't half-a-dozen,' said McGrath.

'We don't want any information from you. We have the situation in hand.'

Frustrated at not being taken seriously, Curnock hung up and began to call the navy when the first swarm of Zeros dropped their bombs. Ear-splitting bombs fell again and again and again. Everywhere, what they described as *nip* planes.

The next morning, trucks picked up the dead and drove them to Mindil Beach where hundreds of bodies were waiting to be buried. With not enough functioning equipment to bury the corpses in time, stray dogs feasted on the carcasses, now flyblown and so bloated in the heat they looked too big for their clothes. Faces had changed. They were taut as balloons, turning from grey to purple, then in time to black.

Jock had spent the night in the shell of the Bank of New South Wales building in Smith Street. Windows had exploded and half the roof had been blown away. He cleared broken glass, twisted metal and sheets of timber to find a spot at the back of a wall where he could rest. The brick building was the safest place to shelter for the night. A sign, *CASHMANS* written in large letters, rested on the shop next door. Sheets of corrugated iron lay on the roof of the veranda.

He didn't sleep. The slightest movement caused pain from the burns and he was on alert for more attacks. At daybreak, the sound of gunfire alarmed him. He soon realised the shooting was ground-fire and he crept along on his stomach taking the tops off blisters on his thighs, shins and arms. He peered through a hole in the wall that had once been a window. Through a cloud of dust, he saw a provost martial driving an army jeep with the canvas top ripped and blowing in the wind as if a half-mast flag. A military policeman stood in the passenger seat hanging onto the windscreen, shooting into the air. Jock kept out of sight and waited until they passed, then crept out into the street – hungry, thirsty, confused and on his own again.

Further along the road, more provosts carted out fridges, foodstuffs, furniture, radios and linen from empty houses. While the household goods were stacked into canvas-covered army trucks, armed guards stood on the footpath. Jock walked on; more looting took place in other parts of town. Police and soldiers scavenged household items. We're in shock, Jock thought as he watched people dazed, ignoring the looting around them.

On the way back to his barracks, Jock caught up to a couple of Royal Australian Air Force men. Their uniforms were torn, their skin scratched and blackened. One had a bandaged arm in a sling made from an air force shirt.

'Where you off to?' asked Jock.

'Orders are to walk half a mile along the road to Adelaide River, then half a mile into the bush,' said the one with his arm in the sling.

'That's right, then we're to stay put and they'll come and give us food and water and tell us what to do next,' said the other. He wiped his brow with the sleeve of his shirt and waved his arm in the direction of the town. 'Not safe in there, mate. There's looting and the provosts have taken over the place and they're as mad as blazes.' He looked at his friend who was nodding in agreement.

'Last night, they were drinking at what was left of The Don, walking through streets, drinking out of bottles and shooting at signs, headlights out of vehicles, pieces of corrugated iron, anything…'

'You'd be safer with us, mate,' said the other.

'No thanks, trying to get to Winnellie. I'll keep going, thanks all the same.' Jock waved and walked on.

There was no direction coming from the Administrator, Aubrey Abbott. Earlier on, Jock had seen him and his wife driving along the road to Adelaide River. Wooden boxes filled their car and were tied to the roof.

The barracks were deserted when he got there; not a soul was around. Jock looked for water and food first and saw how Winnellie had taken its fair share of battering from the raids. A number of buildings were still standing, though others had been flattened. He found what was left of the kitchen and helped himself to fresh water and tins of sardines. He hadn't eaten or had water for nearly two days. He rested on a piece of rubble in the shade of one of the few trees left standing, ate, drank and wondered what to do next.

'Oi Jock, got a drink for a couple of old mates?'

Tic and Horry walked out of a shattered building at the far end of the barracks. They were dirty and their uniforms were torn. Other than that, Jock was pleased to see they were in good shape.

'Well there's a sight for sore eyes,' Jock said.

'We thought you might come back here,' said Tic.

'Just like a battered old homin' pigeon,' said Horry with a big grin on his face.

Jock was pleased to be the focus of Horry's insults again.

'Orders were to go bush,' said Tic.

'Go bush,' said Jock. 'A couple of RAAFies said they were told to go a mile along the road and half a mile in the bush and to stay put.'

'Nah mate!' said Horry as he kicked a piece of rubble on the ground. 'You've got it wrong. The orders are just to go bush. They came from a digger who got the order from someone at the RAAF base, who got it from someone else. It was for everyone, not just RAAFies.'

'Going bush doesn't give me confidence we will be found and given food and water,' Jock said. He pointed to what was left of the kitchen. 'We have food and enough water here for a while, so there is no benefit to traipsing off into the bush. I say we stay put until rations run out and then decide what happens next. Orders may have come through by then.'

Tic and Horry nodded in agreement. While they were the same rank, Jock's maturity took over and the two younger men looked up to him.

As day three broke, Jock, Tic and Horry walked into town to help, moving rubble and throwing it into trucks to be carted away. The streets in the central part of the settlement were covered in debris and Jock knew it was important to have cleared routes for defence force vehicles and ambulances.

The provosts were drunk, unpredictable and violent. They made Jock nervous and he kept out of their way. There was talk that the military police had put officers around the town to halt anyone leaving. At the railway station, they stopped men boarding the trains and shot above their heads yelling insults at them. The provosts tried to turn back civilians but were too late, people had taken off.

Jock had seen crowds on the road south to Adelaide River. Army trucks, jeeps, and civilian cars stacked with suitcases, radios, chairs – whatever could be tied to the top of a car. People walked as cars were filled to the brim with whatever possible. Prams filled with saucepans, clothes, books, and lampshades were pushed. Even wheelbarrows were used to cart luggage and household goods.

'What will happen now?' asked Horry, looking directly at Jock. 'The essential services are damaged or destroyed. Everyone's pissed off to Adelaide River. You should see them traipsing along the road. They're covered in red dust. It's fucking hot, not a skerrick of shade and not much water either.'

'Not a skerrick,' echoed Tic.

'We'll stay put at Winnellie until we receive further orders,' said Jock.

Jock was relieved when orders arrived from Canberra to put the army back in charge of the town. Officers were ordered to round up the soldiers and air force men who had complied with the 'go bush' command. Many had returned to town on their own due to hunger and thirst. Many took the opportunity to desert. Soldiers were found as far away as Melbourne.

The recently promoted Lieutenant Colonel R. B. Hone was put in command of the 2/14th Australian Field Regiment. He stood over six feet tall and weighed twenty stone; behind his back, his men nicknamed him Wimpy. One of his first actions after the initial bombing was to sign transfer papers for two of his gunners of Chinese origin to bases in the south. Their families were market gardeners and the two boys had grown up in Darwin and attended local schools. Hone's concern was that in the event of a ground force invasion by the Japanese, the two might be mistaken for the enemy.

The Lieutenant Colonel kept his men busy. He needed a fit, robust unit for the tropical climate when the order came to go to New Guinea. He wanted to keep them from speculating too much. It was thought that the enemy would employ a land-based invasion and if that was the case he knew the unit was defenceless; his men knew that too. He worked them hard. Jock, Tic and Horry were part of a working party directed to salvage artillery. With the Royal Australian Air Force Base deserted, the regiment borrowed a Vickers machine gun and a Browning Aircraft machine gun to boost its arsenal.

3 MARCH 1942

Now that Hone's been put in charge, there is order in the place. He's working us to the bone and the lads are exhausted – including me. We're woken before sparrows and don't finish until dark. Wimpy said a beer bottle is a handy weapon in a fight. Best you go find yourselves a couple, he said. You may need them because we're staying in Darwin. I'm not confident broken glass would scare the *nips* in planes.

Armed with short-angle iron pickets and eighty rifles, the regiment took over the responsibility for the Royal Australian Air Force Aerodrome ground defence. They were dispersed around the perimeter of the bases at Bagot and Winnellie.

When Jock enlisted, Bess and Cleary moved back into Clarence Street with Mary, Tilly and Honor. Cleary flourished in a house full of doting women. His mother, grandmother or an aunt were always there to make him a sandwich, kiss a skinned knee better or read him a story.

Bess and the baby took over the sunroom at the back of the house. They slept together in a double bed facing the back garden. Green floral curtains hung over louvre windows. A hotchpotch of small rugs covered the green, yellow and blue speckled linoleum.

A bamboo rocking chair stuffed with saggy crocheted-covered cushions sat in one corner. It caught the morning sun. The bedroom was filled with a mixture of women's clothes, creams and the little boy's toys. Opaque French doors led out to the garden. An internal glass door with a yellow floral curtain elasticised top and bottom opened into the lounge room.

When the news came through, Bess had been settling Cleary. Honor opened the sunroom's door and whispered, 'Bess, leave him, come now.'

'But I'm...'

'Now, Bess, now!'

The sisters rushed into the lounge room in time to hear:

This morning mainland Australia came under attack when Japanese forces mounted two air raids on Darwin. It is not known how many were killed or wounded. Aircraft were destroyed; ships anchored in the harbour were sunk, and most civil and military facilities in Darwin were destroyed.

Bess stood by the mantelpiece facing the radio. Close to collapsing, she leaned against the back of the couch. It was a while before she realised Mary had her arm around her shoulders. 'Bess, love, I'm sure Jock will be fine. He's a trained soldier.' Cleary cried. Bess moved to go to him. 'Tilly's with him. He'll settle in a minute.'

The women listened to the wireless late into the night, in the expectation more Darwin news might come through. Bess re-read Jock's letters. She'd glued segments left from the censor's slashing onto writing paper. When the broadcast ceased for the night, she crept into bed and curled her body around Cleary, resting her cheek on his soft hair. Her breathing fell in time with his as they slept, entwined.

In an effort to beat the heat of the day, Bess took Cleary out in the pram early the next morning. Even at that time, the air was warm and she was glad she'd packed their togs. As they passed the Eastern Beach kiosk, she read the day's headlines behind the wire frame: *DARWIN DIGGERS SHOW JAPS WHO'S BOSS.*

At the pool, she found a spot under a tree and spread out the blanket. She lifted Cleary out of his pram and carried him to the children's pool. Other mothers had the same idea and the pool was crowded with children of all ages splashing and laughing. She bobbed Cleary in the water and he giggled when water splashed his face. 'You're growing up far too soon, young man,' she said and hugged him tight.

Drenched and cool, she held Cleary's hand as they walked back to their blanket. On the other side of the tree, a woman with five children had spread their belongings on the ground. The older girls ran to the water with the two younger boys following. Bess didn't recognise the woman as a local and as she approached it was obvious the woman had been crying.

'Gidday,' Bess said. 'It's going to be a scorcher today, I reckon.'

The woman dabbed her eyes. 'This isn't hot for me. I'm from Darwin and it's much hotter up there.'

'Darwin, my husband's in Darwin.'

The woman looked up. Bess noticed her bloodshot and puffy eyes. 'My Bert hasn't written for weeks and I have grave fears something has happened to him in the bombing.'

From a distance she appeared young. Her bright floral, strappy sun-frock was different from the short-sleeved, waisted dresses the local women wore. She had kicked off her sandals and curled one leg beneath her.

'Do you mind if I sit with you?' asked Bess. She spread out her towel and sat on the ground with Cleary on her lap. 'I'm Bess Connor, my Jock's in the 2/14th. It's been a while since I've had word and when I do receive a letter it has been cut to smithereens.'

'I'm Dorothy Lawson. My daughter Peggy and I were evacuated in December.' Bess looked over at the four children playing together. 'Oh, the older girl and the two boys and Ed, this little fella here, were on the ship on their own. I've sort of adopted them.'

The two women chatted until the heat of the day forced them to pack up and return to the cool of indoors.

The next day, Dorothy had arrived at the foreshore first and called out when she saw Bess wheeling the pram along the path. Dorothy was sitting in the shade, near the water and a sandpit. Bess settled herself, peeled a banana, broke it in half and handed a piece each to Ed and Cleary. She pulled out a thermos of cool lemonade and two cups.

'Do you know many people in Geelong, Dorothy?' Bess asked as she filled the beakers.

'We are staying with my husband's cousin and his family, and they have introduced me to a few people and I am working part-time at the Ford factory, so I know a few folk there too,' said Dorothy. 'Haven't made many friends, though.'

'Well you have now,' said Bess as she handed her a cup of cool lemonade.

'I hope so.'

The two women sat in silence while watching the older children play in the pool and Cleary and Ed digging in the sandpit with the other kids.

'What's Darwin like?' Bess asked.

Dorothy leaned her head back against the tree and watched fine white clouds scud across the sky. She talked of the town's wide dusty streets, Chinatown, the Star Theatre and Winnellie Barracks where Jock was stationed. Dorothy was lost in thought as she talked of her hometown and Bess recognised her friend's sadness at being so far away from loved ones and friends.

'I'm intrigued how you made it to Geelong from Darwin?'

'We were made to leave,' Dorothy said as she pulled her blonde hair back and tied it up with a scarf. 'It wasn't our decision. We didn't want to go. A week before we left there was a Decree handed down by the Administrator, Aubrey Abbott. It was published in the newspaper ordering women and children to leave for the southern states. We had no choice.'

Around midnight, two soldiers carrying torches, with thin pieces of cloth tied over the lights, knocked on the front door of Bert and Dorothy Lawson's house. Hessian bags tacked over windows dimmed the glow from kerosene lamps hanging inside. Bert opened the screen door but could barely make out the figures in the dark. Beery breath caused him to turn his face away and wave his hand in a faint effort to disperse the odour.

Ten-year-old Peggy woke to the sound of footsteps on the timber veranda and the familiar squeak of the flywire door. Sleepy-eyed, she walked down the hall to the lounge room. Standing in the doorway with her one-eyed teddy bear squashed under her arm, she watched her parents embrace. Her father's big arms enveloped her mother who was quietly crying on his shoulder.

'Who were those men? What's happening?' Peggy asked.

Dorothy sat on the couch. She drew Peggy onto her lap and said, 'Those men are soldiers, and they came to tell us to pack our bags and be ready to be picked up tomorrow morning.' As she spoke, she stroked her daughter's hair. 'Then they will drive you and me to the wharf and we will sail down south so we will be safe in case the Japanese attack the town.'

'What about Daddy?' Peggy looked at her father standing above them. Bert sat on the couch next to his wife and daughter and put his arm around the two of them.

'I will stay here to protect our house and the town against the Japanese. I'll be fine, love. They won't hurt me.'

'I don't want to go!'

'We have to. It will be like an adventure,' said Dorothy.

'Will there be kids for me to play with?'

Dorothy held Peggy's hand. 'Of course, I am sure there will be some of your friends on the ship and you will make lots of new friends wherever we go.'

'I still don't want to go.'

'We must, Peggy. It won't be for long. We'll be back before you know it.'

'I will miss Daddy. What about Fluffy, can I take her?'

'No. Cats won't be allowed on the ship.'

'Fluffy can keep me company,' said Bert. 'Fluffy and I are mates.'

Peggy began to cry. 'I don't want to go.'

Dorothy hugged her tightly. 'It's final, we must, Peg. Go and pack some of your dollies and Ted in your school satchel and then you will have them with you.'

'What about my books?'

'Just one or two small ones. Not too much. I'll pack your clothes with mine.'

By nine o'clock, the blazing sun stung heads and uncovered flesh. A steady stream of trucks and jeeps dropped off more women and children. Bodies pushed together on the pier made the air even more stifling, hampering any hint of a sea breeze. With no water available, dehydration was taking its toll. Pregnant women sat on suitcases; some rested their heads in their hands, others fanned themselves with handkerchiefs. Mothers tried in vain to placate grizzling babies and children.

Edna Davies had three kids under eleven and their faces were beet-red. The youngest was wilting in her arms; tiny droplets of sweat covered his face and forehead. Edna saw a guard standing at the end of the wharf and moved through the crowd towards him. 'Please bring us some water? The children are perishing in this relentless heat, and so are the adults.'

He pulled the brim of his hat down so he couldn't see her. She looked at the water bottle hanging from his belt. 'We need some water. This is cruel.'

The guard looked the other way.

It was a hundred in the shade with nowhere to hide from the scorching sun beating down on the wharf. Eyes stung from the sun's glare on the water.

Around midday, the women were told to board the *Zealandia*. Dorothy and Peggy walked along the gangplank. Peg watched the murky water through the gaps between the wooden slats. As she went to step onto the ship, the guard stood between mother and daughter, looming over the little girl.

'What's in your bag, love?'

'My dollies.'

He opened Peggy's leather satchel, pushed one doll into her hand then threw her opened bag and its contents into the water. Peggy hung onto the handrail on tiptoes sobbing as her beloved toys and books plopped one after the other into the water.

'Did you have to do that?' Dorothy asked.

'Keep moving.'

They found a place on the deck close to the railing. Dorothy put the suitcase flat on the boards for her daughter to stand on. Peggy looked down into the foam and saw her two dolls bobbing up and down before sinking feet first. The waves banged her one-eyed teddy bear against the side of the ship before it eventually became waterlogged and submerged. Her books floated for a while before sinking. She was pleased she left Fluffy safe at home.

In the killer heat, without water or food, the women and children crammed onto the decks. Metal surfaces radiated heat. Skin blistered. Sick or pregnant women gravitated towards thin bands of welcome shade.

Eventually, the long-awaited sea breeze arrived. Women turned their faces upwards and closed their eyes, embracing the relief.

Parish Priest, Father Goy, drove up to the wharf in his open-tray truck with boxes of fruit for the women and children. He walked up the gangplank wearing shorts and an open-neck shirt. His arms were filled with two wooden cases overflowing with fresh produce. Before he stepped onto the ship, a guard took the cartons of oranges, apples and mangoes from the priest and threw them into the water.

'No food allowed to be taken on board. We have been told only the bare essentials are allowed, Father.'

Under the guise of not overloading the ship, provosts randomly threw personal belongings overboard: family treasures, suitcases filled with clothes and photo albums, framed pictures, biscuit tins filled with photographs and trinkets. Many women had babies and small children, yet prams were not permitted.

Before the ship set sail, ballast bags had to be used to balance the vessel as it was deemed too light.

It was late afternoon by the time the *Zealandia* slid out of the dock. Five hundred and forty-two women and children, two hundred sick troops picked up in Singapore, one hundred and seven crew and one hundred Japanese internees were jammed in together.

Bert stood with the other men on the small hill near the wharf. Peggy kept her eyes on her father, held her remaining doll up high and made its hand wave at him. Bert waved back and blew kisses to his wife and daughter until they became tiny specks in the distance. Dorothy held back tears as she held her hand up high, and swayed it back and forth. How am I going to look after us? We have one suitcase, twenty pounds and I don't know whether there'll be anyone to meet us at the other end.

When the shore became just a speck on the horizon, Dorothy and Peggy were herded into a group with other women and children and ordered to follow a thick-set man. He had tattoos on his arms and wore a white shirt and pants stained with black grease. He led them down three levels of narrow winding stairs. At each descent, the air became more stifling and hot. When they reached the bottom deck, he allocated cabins without any order or thought.

'You lot sleep in there,' he said to two women with six children between them.

He signalled for the rest of the group to follow, then opened another compartment door. 'You mob in there,' he waved to a mother with a limp red-faced child in her arms and four children crowded around her. 'You too,' he said to a pregnant woman with two children.

She protested. 'There are only four bunks! That's not enough room for all of us.'

The sailor ignored her and kept walking, allotting sleeping quarters without any thought about the consequences. At the end of the passageway, only Dorothy and Peggy remained. They turned left into a corridor, narrower than the first.

'You two in there,' said the sailor then turned on his heel and walked away.

Dorothy and Peg's cabin had two sets of double bunks, a small table and two floor-to-ceiling skinny cupboards built up close to the beds. The room was airless, dank and smelled of urine. On one of the bottom beds sat a girl of about fifteen with her legs crossed and a small boy on her lap. Two boys were on the top bunk. Their arms were wrapped around their knees and they had squashed themselves flat against the wall.

'Hello. I'm Dorothy and this is Peggy.'

'I'm Dawn, this is Ed,' the girl said as she put her arms tighter around the little boy. She pointed her right index finger up to the top bunk and said, 'Harry and Reg.'

Dorothy noticed the children's grubby faces and clothes and how their hair needed a good wash and brush.

'Where's your mother?'

'I don't know,' said Dawn.

'Is she on the ship?'

'No, she cleared off months ago.'

'Did your Daddy bring you to the ship?'

'No, we don't know where he is either.'

Peggy looked up at her mother. Dorothy looked down at her daughter's clean face and shiny hair.

'Well, who looks after you?'

'I do,' said Dawn. 'And sometimes we go over to Mrs Hudson's.'

'Is Mrs Hudson on this ship?'

'I haven't seen her. I don't know where she is.' Tears formed in the girl's eyes. 'Soldiers came around early this morning and told us to get in the truck. They said the yellow peril was coming and they'd torture and kill us and we had to get on the ship.'

Japanese women and children who had been living in Darwin were put into the hold with the Japanese internees and forbidden to mix with Anglos. They were locked away except for supervised trips for fresh air. On day two, when the soldiers herded the Japanese women and children onto the deck for their dose of sunlight, Peggy saw her school friend Yuki walking, head downcast, behind her mother.

'Yuki, Yuki, it's me, Peggy.'

The Japanese girl lifted her head, smiled and waved.

'I'm glad you're here,' said Peggy and tried to run to her friend. She was stopped by a guard holding a gun across his chest. It was the one who had tossed the contents of her satchel into the water. Dorothy learned his name was O'Reilly.

'You can't mix with the prisoners. These Japs could be spies.'

Peggy looked up at the soldier. 'Yuki's not a spy. She's my friend. We sit together at school.'

The little girl tried to step around the provost, and he moved in the same direction, blocking her path. She stepped to the other side. The soldier did the same. Peggy looked up at the guard and poked her tongue out. He pushed her on the shoulder. 'Move back to where you were and stay away from the prisoners.'

She ran back to where her mother was standing with the other women and buried her head into Dorothy's chest. 'Why is Yuki and her family prisoners Mum? They're not spies.'

Dorothy placed an arm around Peggy and said under her breath, 'You'll keep, O'Reilly, you'll keep.'

That night, Dorothy soaked the hard biscuits in lukewarm tea to soften them for Peggy, Dawn and her brothers to eat. Harry and Peggy were about the same age and the next day they took Reg with them and played with the other children on the ship.

Dorothy held Ed on her lap as she sat on the deck and the women made themselves comfortable. They upturned wooden crates and used them as seats. Many women had children a similar age to Ed and the little ones played together in the safety of the women who were always close by.

Dawn was never too far away and Dorothy felt the girl enjoyed relying on a responsible adult. While they cleaned the cabin together, Dawn told her how both her parents had spent their waking hours drinking and fighting until they passed out, only to start again the next day.

'I've been looking after the boys for as long as I can remember,' she said. 'Being on this ship is easier for me than at home. We are being looked after here. I don't want us to get off,' she said and began to cry. 'I don't know where we'll go or what we'll do.'

'It's okay, love. You don't have to make that decision yet,' said Dorothy, not knowing herself what the future would hold.

———————

Dorothy dreaded the nights. No lights were allowed on board and portholes were blackened, which meant everyone went to bed at sundown. It was too dangerous to move around in the dark. Settling five children in the small, airless cabin meant crying nearly every night.

She knew it could be worse and was pleased the children were well. With the shortage of baby food, many small children were sick, which meant their mothers were confined to cabins, nursing ill youngsters twenty-four hours a day.

'Do you have family in Melbourne, Dottie?' asked Edna. Dorothy noticed the seams of Edna's dress weren't under as much pressure as when she first boarded the ship. Everyone was losing weight quickly. The only food on offer was the bully beef and biscuits and the briny water upset people's stomachs. Many complained of diarrhoea.

'I know no-one in Victoria,' she replied. 'My Bert has a distant cousin who lives in Geelong. After he had waved us off, he was going to the post office to send a telegram telling him of our arrival date – which is a guess anyway.'

On Christmas Day, lunch was served in the dining room. Dorothy, Edna and their children, Dawn and her brothers sat at a long table with bench seats. The crew entered the dining hall carrying big trays of plates filled with steamed chicken and potatoes followed by jelly and custard. The children clapped their hands and the adults cheered.

'A feast,' said Edna. 'Real food.'

Dorothy sat back and watched adults and children laugh and chat. Such a different mood from the bully beef meals, she thought.

Days later, they berthed at Bowen in Queensland.

'I can't wait to set foot on solid ground,' Dorothy said to Peggy. 'Go and fetch Dawn and the boys and we'll walk into Bowen together.'

She followed the children down the gangplank and was struck by the brightness of the tall palm trees, banana trees and lush gardens. After days of looking at different hues of the ocean and blue sky, foliage took on a luminescent tone. Houses were built on stilts with wide wraparound verandas. Gardens were framed with untamed giant red, orange and yellow bougainvillea.

Dawn, Peggy, Reg and Harry raced one another along a dirt road in front of Dorothy piggybacking Ed. The children were thrilled with being able to run in a straight line as opposed to a circular direction on a crowded slippery, timber deck. Women holding baskets of fruit and wearing identical pinafores with the letters CWA embroidered in lemon cotton over their right breast met passengers along the road.

'Here you go, kiddies,' one said as she handed the children an orange each.

'Thank God, fresh fruit,' Dot said as she thanked the women.

Alerted to the evacuees' arrival, residents opened up their homes with invitations to a meal and a friendly chat. Dorothy wanted to make the most of walking on firm ground and to look at the shops. She knew the children would benefit from running in the fresh air, so declined the invitation. She found a sweet shop and bought a bag of barley sugar. She took her time in the fruit shop, picking out the best quality fruit. After paying her money she left with bags of oranges and apples, enough for each child to have a piece of fruit daily until they disembarked at Port Melbourne. Any left over she would leave with Dawn and her brothers. What would become of her and the three little tykes? Dawn was just a kid herself.

When the time came to return, she gathered up her charges for the walk back to the jetty. The children looked tired, but Dorothy could tell by their faces they were relaxed for the first time since boarding the *Zealandia*. She wondered whether Dawn and her brothers ever looked this calm. The tightness around their eyes had gone and they laughed and played like normal children.

O'Reilly stood at the top of the gangplank. Dorothy carried her shopping bags filled with fruit and sweets for the children. She walked up the ramp with the five youngsters in a single line behind her. O'Reilly wrenched the bags out of her hands and smashed them with a baton. Squashed to a pulp, juice from the oranges dripped through the hessian causing sticky puddles to form on the deck.

Peggy, Reg, Harry and Ed began to cry. Dawn picked up the toddler.

'What are you doing?' Dorothy asked, horrified.

'We don't want any alcohol brought on board the ship. We know you women have been sneaking grog on.'

Dorothy took a step closer to the guard, pushed her face forward so she was a few inches from his face. 'You have just smashed fruit and lollies I bought for the children. Are you all mad?'

'That's enough from you, misses, get moving.' He handed the bags back to her.

Dorothy felt pressure in her chest and began to breathe deeply. The events of the last few weeks built up within her: the dire days on the ship; leaving her Bert behind; Peggy's dolls thrown into the ocean; the bully beef; the salt water; not knowing where she was going or what she would do; spending precious money from her twenty pounds on fruit and sweets for the children, only to have them smashed. She moved even closer to the guard and stared into his eyes. They were the meanest eyes Dorothy had ever seen. At another time they would have intimidated her and she would have backed away.

'Keep them, you stupid drongo.'

Dorothy didn't blink and thought: if you so much as move your mouth the wrong way, I will kill you with my bare hands.

She watched the veins in the guard's neck bulge and pulse.

'Eat them yourself. I hope you choke and die a painful death and I hope I'm around to see it,' she said. 'You make me sick. Rot in hell.' A piece of spit shot out of her mouth and landed on O'Reilly's cheek. She held his stare.

He placed the sodden hessian bags gently on the ground and stepped aside so she could pass. She stood with her back to him and ushered her brood onto the ship for the last leg of the journey.

There was no-one to meet Dorothy and Peggy when they docked at Port Melbourne a few days later. They sheltered in a building on the wharf with other women and children waiting to be met. On the third day, a man walked up the wharf yelling, 'Lawson, Lawson, I'm looking for Dorothy Lawson.'

She stood up and waved her hat. 'I'm Dorothy Lawson. I'm Bert's wife.'

Maurie Lawson stood six foot four with broad shoulders. His face was weathered. A wide-brimmed hat was pulled down to shade his face. He stood with his legs apart and smiled. Dorothy could see a faint resemblance between her husband and the man in front of her. The same smile, the same round face.

A tall woman in a yellow cotton frock and straw hat stepped forward and kissed Dorothy on the cheek. Smiling, she said, 'Hello Dorothy, I'm Shirley, Maurie's wife. We've been looking forward to your visit.'

'The date on Bert's telegram had been cut out,' Maurie said as he picked up the case. 'It was a guess as to when you'd arrive. I heard a ship had docked when I drove into town. I thought there were just the two of you.'

'There were at the beginning of the trip. But these children have nowhere to go.'

'Fair enough,' said Shirley. 'We'll work something out, won't we kids?'

Bess' life revolved around looking after her son, sewing clothes on a treadle machine, gardening and cooking. In the evening, when Cleary was in bed asleep, she spent her time writing letters to Jock, not knowing whether they'd reach him or not, reading, or playing canasta with her sisters and mother with the wireless humming, just in case there was news.

Bess and Cleary continued to spend time with Dorothy and the children. The weather had changed; a late autumn chill was in the air. Trees were changing colour to vibrant reds and oranges, and regular rain turned the parched ground into lush grass. The colours of the autumnal trees fascinated Dorothy, so different from Darwin's tropical weather all year long. On fine days the two women and their children walked along the foreshore or through Geelong's Botanic Gardens where the older children kicked autumn leaves and played games together. The two little ones, Ed and Cleary, played alongside one another on a blanket while the women stretched out, read or chatted. Letters from Darwin were nearly non-existent now. Both women lived in hope and checked their mailboxes daily.

One day, when Bess turned into Clarence Street, she saw a bike parked against their front fence. A serviceman stood on the front porch. From the back she thought it might be Jock and her heart knocked against her chest, but when the soldier turned side-on she realised it wasn't.

'Can I help you?' asked Bess.

'I'm looking for Mary Brown.'

Mary appeared in the doorway wringing her hands on the bottom of her apron. Her eyes fixed on the telegram. She looked at Bess and swayed slightly before collapsing on the front step.

The message read: *Died on Active Service*. Frank had been killed at Ambon.

Sadness hung over Clarence Street and this time Mary was inconsolable. She took to her bed. Honor and Tilly followed suit. With a toddler to look after, Bess wasn't afforded the luxury of nursing her grief through rest and sleep. The heartache from losing her little brother overwhelmed her. She missed Jock more than ever and wished life could go back to the time before Robert Menzies had addressed the nation.

Dorothy received a letter from Darwin. Bert had been killed in the first bombing attack. At first, Dorothy didn't tell Peggy, but when the little girl found the letter, she stopped talking, eating, refused to go to school and stayed in her bedroom. Reg and Harry couldn't understand why she didn't want to play. They didn't understand the heartbreak of losing a loving parent. To them, it was a relief when their father left.

Dawn took over the running of the house. She had learned from Dorothy the importance of a domestic rhythm. She cooked the meals, cleaned the house, ensured the boys were bathed and in bed on time. She made broth for Dorothy and Peggy and took trays to their rooms only to retrieve the uneaten soup at a later time.

In winter, Bess and Dorothy's meetings in the park and on the foreshore stalled. They agreed the weather was too cold to take the children out. The unspoken truth was they both needed to stay indoors to tend to their grief.

Dorothy found a house in Clarence Street where she and the children could live on their own. It was near Bess and the older children's school. While Dorothy worked at the Ford factory, Bess looked after Ed. Through heartbreak and loneliness, the women worked together to make a life for themselves and their children.

After eighteen months in Darwin, Jock was given leave and spent two weeks with Bess and Cleary. Time in Geelong with his wife and son restored him. Hand in hand, they strolled along Eastern Beach with their three-year-old running around their legs. They attended a couple of dances at the Geelong Town Hall. Bess borrowed one of Honor's frocks – a short-sleeved, navy-blue waisted dress with white collar and cuffs. She pinched her lips to give them colour and sprayed herself with lavender water she kept for a special occasion. Jock polished his boots and wore his soldier's uniform.

With her dance card discarded, Bess enjoyed every precious dance with her husband. The band played their favourites, *The Andrews Sisters'* 'Boogie Woogie Bugle Boy of Company B', 'Chattanooga Choo Choo' and 'Well All Right', taking them back to an easier time, innocent days of prewar courtship. Jock was relieved and excited being separated hadn't robbed them of their ease with one another. Each anticipated the other as they glided around the dance floor.

The youngster slept in one of the front bedrooms with either his grandmother or one of his aunts. Cleary protested loudly, slid out of bed and ran to the sunroom to find the door locked. He could hear his parents' voices on the other side of the wall.

'He's used to sleeping with me. He doesn't understand.'

'Well, he has to learn. My place is in bed with you. That's the way it will be when I'm home for good, so he may as well learn now.'

Bess lay quietly in the dark holding her husband's hand. There was a sternness about him that hadn't been there before. In time, someone took the sobbing boy back to bed. Jock raised himself onto his right elbow, smiled and stroked Bess' hair.

'He may come back.'

'We've just over a week, love, before I go. Can we...?'

For a fortnight, they lived as a family in the small cottage with thin walls. The lack of privacy was frustrating for Jock. He had dreamed of his time with Bess. What he hadn't taken into consideration were her mother, sisters and their son. Moments alone with his wife were few. Early mornings were the best. In the quiet house, he relished the touch of her soft, smooth body lying next to him. But the three-year-old was often at the door banging and kicking before one of the women in the house distracted him.

Breakfast, lunch and tea were eaten at the kitchen table with Mary, Tilly, Honor and Cleary. Jock breathed in the smells of home-cooked meals, lavender water and velvet soap, a welcome contrast to the pong of men's sweaty socks, Craven As and days' old perspiration. He took in the ordinary household aromas, trying to file them away so he could retrieve them when he was back with his unit – a photograph of the senses.

He mowed the lawns, changed light globes and replaced washers in leaky taps. Bess laundered her husband's army shirts with her son's clothes in giant cement troughs in the lean-to at the back of the house. She filled a metal bucket with cold water then dropped in a Reckitt's laundry blue bag. She swished Jock's grubby singlets around in the blue-black water and left them to soak for a good few hours, before hanging them on the washing line strung between the side of the house and the trellis. She was proud of the now snowy-white singlets.

Jock found a pile of newspapers in the wastepaper stack at the back of the laundry. He folded a piece in half, then half again, then half again until he had an oblong shape. He placed this on another piece of newspaper, folded over both ends and wrapped the inner rectangular piece similar to a parcel of fish and chips. He continued until he had what resembled a curved rectangle-shaped football. He wound string around and around then secured it. Jock smiled, pleased with his make-do football.

'Watch this, son.'

The boy was sitting in the sandpit digging with his red spade, plopping sand into a small tin bucket with red sailboats on the side. Jock dropped the newspaper football onto his foot and kicked it, softly.

He picked it up and said, 'Watch again,' then repeated the kick.

'Come on, son.' Jock took Cleary's hand, stood him up, walked him out of the sandpit onto the lawn and placed the newspaper football into his hands. 'You have a go, mate.' The son looked up at his father.

'Kick it, like I did. Come on, kick it like I showed you. Go on, have a go. Kick it, kick it, as I showed you.' Jock took the newspaper football out of Cleary's hands and dropped it onto his foot and gave it a gentle kick. 'See, it's easy.'

It was too much for the little boy and ended in tears.

'Now don't cry. That's silly. Don't be a baby. Come on, kick it,' and Jock pushed the newspaper football into the little boy's chest.

Bess watched while she hung out the second load of washing. She noticed how Jock's speech was sounding more Australian – his English accent softening. In addition, she noticed how impatient he had become.

She walked over and stood next to Cleary and put her arm around his shoulder. He buried his face in her dress. She patted his head and stroked the side of his face.

'Never mind, there, there. It's alright.'

Jock watched his wife and son together. He'd never have the bond they had. He remembered again the last conversation he'd had with his own mother and the familiar sense of dread and aloneness returned.

Cleary stopped crying and Bess handed Jock a red rubber ball.

'Throw this to him, but not too hard. He can manage that.'

Jock had wanted to be close to his son, had looked forward to seeing him again after the years away. He had missed out on so much of the boy's growing up.

'Give him time, love,' Bess said. 'He doesn't know who you are. You left when he was just months old. It's not his fault you're a stranger to him. You're the one who made the decision to leave. Didn't you think there'd be consequences to such a choice?'

'I don't have time. I've only got a few days left.' Jock stood holding the rubber ball in one hand. 'He's being spoiled here with you women. He's growing up to be a sissy. He can't even kick a football.'

'He's not yet four. Hardly a failure if he can't kick a football.'

'Well, it's got to change when I'm home for good.' Jock threw the ball into the sandpit and walked up the path to the back door. 'There will be rules he has to obey.'

Bess moved back to the clothesline. Cleary walked with her holding her dress. 'Rules! What are you talking of, rules?' Bess said. 'This is not the bloody army.'

She had become the go-between, translating their son's wants for Jock and comforting the boy when his father expected too much. To keep the peace, she took to lying next to the youngster at night-time in the front bedroom until he drifted off to sleep. Jock played canasta in the lounge room with her mother and sisters.

When her son's breathing indicated he was asleep, she untangled herself and crept out of the room. She walked along the hallway to the lounge room to where the canasta game was taking place and stood in the doorway trying to adjust her eyes to the brightness of the room.

Jock smiled when he saw her and said, 'Come and help me out, love. The girls are ganging up on me.'

Lae

Army records, war diaries, veterans' anecdotes and my father's journals helped me piece together my father's time in New Guinea between 1943 and 1945.

Orders arrived for the 2/14th to leave Australia. With America's large contingent of armed forces annihilated in Darwin, New Guinea was strategically important as it provided locations for Japan to set up large land, air and naval bases. The enemy was well and truly entrenched in the jungles and it was the 2/14th's job to stop them advancing. Jock was part of a regiment sent to Lae, to set up camp. Orders were to take over from the men who had been fighting the Japanese in the jungles for months. They were skin and bone and suffering either malaria, dysentery or both.

It was 1943. Jock leaned on the railing of the Dutch merchant ship SS *Bontekoe*. He stared into the pitch-black sky, embracing the fresh ocean air. The diesel odour and the sea breeze took him back to his voyage from Southampton to Melbourne in twenty-nine.

A lifetime ago.

Handrails, seats, windowsills and lumpy pipes were covered with a greasy dark smudge, a mixture of black soot from the *Bontekoe* engines and sea air. Jock wrote there wasn't much difference between the Dutch and British ships. But the passengers and their destinations were worlds apart. His voyage to Australia had been filled with excitement of a new life in a country filled with space, fresh air and sunshine. During the eight-week voyage from Southampton to Melbourne, three babies had been born. In capital letters and underlined twice, he had written *NO BETTER SYMBOL OF NEW BEGINNINGS*.

On the *Bontekoe*, Jock could sense the men, many not yet twenty, knew danger was ahead of them. Dread and anticipation were palpable. Jock wondered whether he'd return and whether he'd return the same. His thoughts were interrupted by the unmistakable noise of someone heaving. He knew what it meant. Many people he'd travelled with from the United Kingdom spent their sea voyage bent over the ship's rail. He followed the sound and came across a young man stripped to his waist leaning over the vessel's handrail.

'Can I get you water, mate?'

'Yeah, I'm out. Dropped mine over the side.'

Jock handed him his water bottle. 'I'm Jock.'

The young man took a gulp, rinsed his mouth then spat over the side. 'Joe Forrester.'

'Takes a while to get sea legs,' said Jock. 'You'll be right.'

Days later Jock saw land – just a speck on the horizon at first. He was on the top deck watching the sea and lost in thoughts of Bess and their son. He missed them and wondered whether he'd see them again. Guilt and dread flooded him when he remembered the way he acted with Cleary. I'm a drongo making him kick a stupid newspaper football. I don't know what I was thinking. He made a promise to himself he'd make it up to his boy next time they were together, by being more patient and not expecting too much from him.

As the ship edged closer, a wall of untamed prehistoric wilderness materialised before his eyes – an ancient landscape of giant trees and thick rainforest. He thought of how ordered England's landscape was compared to the jungle emerging before him. He remembered Bess' garden in Geelong, the fig and lemon trees, lavender bushes, geraniums, arum lilies, and spongy buffalo grass.

He stood in the clearing taking in the verdant landscape surrounding him. Both sides of the Butibum River were edged with snarled forest and hundred-year-old palm trees with umbrella-sized leaves. Pink and orange tropical flowers shot through the soft grass. The air was humid and thick with a scent Jock hadn't come across before – frangipani, a perfect, delicate white flower amidst the rugged terrain. The grass was covered with a carpet of frangipani blossoms. Every now and then a single perfect flower lay in the midst of the bruised and brown petals.

They set up away from the sandy riverbed, hidden in the primitive landscape between two mountain ranges. The locals called the larger group Atzera, the smaller remained nameless. What little clothes Jock wore, were constantly damp from sweat or rain.

Camp was assembled on the soft grass under pandanus palms. Canvas sheets thrown over stripped bamboo poles became two-man shelters. The front and back of the tents were left open to make the most of any breeze, and closed against the pelting rains by unfurling the rolled up canvas sheets. Larger tents housed long tables and benches. The men used these pavilions as a meeting place where they ate their meals, wrote journals or letters home, played card games, or just sat, smoked and talked. A number were fitted out as sleeping quarters. Wooden supply boxes and tin drums were set up outdoors and used as seats and tables. The tents were erected in a horseshoe shape with the central section left for drill practice and parades. Bulky army supply boots killed the grass and the rains created a muddy mess.

Breakfast was the usual weevil-infested bully beef and tinned peaches. Jock couldn't face it again and ate two bananas and a guava he found on the ground, followed by a cup of weak black tea. He threw the fruit scraps at a couple of ravens scavenging near the communal tent, rinsed his mug in a bowl of water and walked back to his tent. He slipped the cup into the folded blanket then checked his gun leaning against a couple of wooden boxes stacked in the corner and made sure his Owen was empty with the safety switch on.

He was reminded of the talk describing the Owen, known as the 'diggers' darling', when they were back at Puckapunyal. The officer-in-charge had explained the benefits of this new weapon, how it was different to similar guns of its type. It had a selector switch. This meant it could be secured in a 'safe' position. If the trigger was pulled, it wouldn't shoot. On setting two, it slipped to semi-automatic, shooting just once. On the last setting, the weapon became fully automatic, shooting multiple times. He made sure the safety switch was on and his gun was empty.

Lieutenant Broom, a new officer assigned to them, reminded Jock of a head prefect at an all-boys private school. While most soldiers were bare-chested with their socks flopping over their boots, Broom had tucked his buttoned-up shirt neatly into his shorts and pulled his socks up to just under his knees, folding each top over so they matched perfectly.

Jock wrote of his curiosity as to what caused such a man to tick. Broom was a loner, rude and disrespectful to the men under his command. Whenever possible, he grovelled to higher-ranked officers. During a card game, Jock heard Broom's story from Bluey. The young gunner and the Lieutenant had grown up in the same street in Glenelg, south of Adelaide. The red-headed soldier punctuated the card game with snippets of Broom, always checking over his shoulder, making sure the Lieutenant was out of earshot. He told the men around the table how Broom's father was a major in the 5th Australian Division in the First World War – one of the five and a half thousand men killed within a twenty-four-hour period at the Battle of Fromelles. Broom was five when his mother received the news. She took the envelope from the telegram man, walked into the lounge room and drank the cocktail cabinet dry then passed out on the floor. Broom joined the army on his eighteenth birthday and when he walked into the kitchen in his uniform his mother burst into tears then opened a bottle of vermouth, or so the story went.

Bluey's mum told her son the reason she thought he had joined up was because he liked knowing what was going to happen next. This was different to home, when his mother could be cooking tea and talking one night and then passed out drunk on the floor, the next.

The Lieutenant stood under the pandanus palms in the middle of the boggy clearing with hands on hips and feet spread wide apart.

He ordered the men to strip bamboo for tent supports.

Jock struggled with cutting the rattan. It was a case of learning as you go. The machete he was given was old and had rusted in the tropical air. He watched the others attack the bamboo, but they weren't much better. He tried holding the stalk at the top and then ran the machete downwards. But he couldn't get traction and the tool slipped and came close to cutting his leg. He swerved to save himself and nicked the side of his hand. As he wrapped his dirty handkerchief around the cut, he heard a rustling noise behind the clumps. He had been looking for older, thicker, bamboo and hadn't realised he'd wandered deep into the jungle away from the other men. He stood stock-still and moved his head from one side to the other, listening, trying to work out what was making the noise. They had been warned of wild boars, how they'd run straight at you, lift you off your feet with their tusks, then come back and gore their startled prey. Plus, the threat of the Japanese nearby was always front of mind.

He had left his Owen leaning next to a tree fifty yards away. He had no hope. The noise grew louder. Whatever was behind the bamboo was moving closer. I'm a goner. His hands began to tremble and he thought of making a run for it when Joe Forrester appeared from the thicket and took the machete out of Jock's hands.

'Here mate, give us a shot.' He stripped the stalk cleanly and quickly, moved onto another, then another, until three identical tent poles lay flattening the kunai grass.

In an attempt to steady his hands, Jock pushed them deep in his pockets and said in a deep voice, 'Well, you're looking better than when I saw you on deck the other night.'

'I'm on solid ground mate, that's why.'

'Pretty deft with that machete.'

'I worked in a timber yard in Perth. Used to working with wood.'

Jock took his sweaty hands out of his pockets and walked towards where Joe was stripping the bamboo.

'Usually, cut logs much thicker than this. That's how I got to Darwin; brought a load up for laying tracks.' He skinned another piece of bamboo and threw it on the ground. Then turned and sliced another at its base, held it at one end, with the other resting on the earth, and continued cutting. 'Got drinking with a few blokes at The Don and before I knew it, I'd joined up. Thanks for the water. It was a lifesaver.'

Jock piled the bamboo together. 'No worries.'

'Always been a healthy bloke; never known such sickness. Glad I didn't enlist in the navy. Probably would have deserted the first port I landed in. You've done a bit of sailing, have you, Jock?'

'From Southampton to Melbourne.'

'Where's that?'

'England, mate,' Jock said smiling to himself.

'This is the furthest I've travelled,' Joe said, as he skinned more bamboo. 'And before here, the furthest was Darwin. I guess you could say I've lived a sheltered life in Perth.'

'Live with family, do you, son?'

'My parents and six brothers; I'm the youngest. Mum was cut up when I sent her a telegram saying I'd enlisted too. The other boys joined up – overseas in Ambon, Malaya and the Dutch East Indies. My sweetheart Cecilia isn't too happy either. She sent me a letter and I could tell she'd been crying when she wrote it.'

'How?'

'She wrote it in the letter.'

Jock smiled again to himself.

'She wants to get married, but me going to Darwin and then enlisting and now over here, that will have to wait.'

'I'm sure she'll get over it, mate,' said Jock. The two men worked together stacking and tying twine around bundles of bamboo.

'Do you have anyone bunking in your tent, Jock?'

Jock shook his head slowly from side to side. 'On my Pat Malone at the moment. Thought I must have had stinky body odour. But then again, I suppose all of us have that.'

'Do you mind if I bunk in with you? I'm in the long tent. It's crowded, noisy.'

'Sure, son. I'm at the end of camp. I'm a quiet lad.'

'Suits me. Might help keep me out of trouble.'

Within days, mould grew on leather boots, kitbags, blankets, hats, clothes, canvas ceilings, and walls. Fresh air moving through the shelters was a weak effort against the multiplying spores. The ground, carpeted with lush grass, was home to snakes, giant spiders and scorpions. Jock made sure his army supply and personal effects were kept up off the ground to stop the marauders from slipping into dark corners. He was in the habit of shaking boots and clothes before dressing, a lesson he learned while stationed in Darwin.

Jock and Joe swapped stories. Joe was intrigued by Jock's life in England and reciprocated by telling Jock of his dream of buying land for a farm, building his own house, marrying Cecilia and having a cricket team of kids.

'I haven't told anyone else this,' Joe said as they worked together building the camp. 'People might think I'm bonkers. Where will I get money to buy a farm and build a house? I'm just a numbskull from Perth.'

'Life's in front of you, lad. It's a great dream to have,' said Jock.

Jock was grateful for Joe's strength when they needed to shift the heavy wireless casings and batteries from ship to camp. Palm trees were used as makeshift towers. Wires were looped from tree to tree in an effort to pick up signals from other camps scattered across the island, or on ships anchored off the coast. New Guinea's rough terrain was a major interference with coverage and the humid conditions disrupted machinery. If the line was dead, it was trial and error to find the cause. Rats were a major culprit as they ate through wires. Jock was one of a number of signalmen whose job it was to send and receive messages. He was in a team of four and worked a six-hour shift, during a twenty-four-hour period, for seven days. Then another team took over. Night shifts were the worst. On your own in the pitch-black was dangerous. Not only could nocturnal animals cause damage, but a number of Papuans were dangerous. While most of the local people were friendly and harmless, there had been cases where men on night duty were found in the morning with their throats slit.

Jock spent much of his spare time writing. He found a couple of old wooden supply boxes and used them as a writing table and seat at the back of his tent, away from the racket of the parade ground and the noise from the other soldiers.

15 NOVEMBER 1943

Settled into camp life here in the wilds of NG. Joe Forrester has attached himself to me and I can tell he is missing home and the closeness of his big family. He talks a lot of home back in Perth, his mum and dad and brothers. None of the other lads listen to him and tell him to wipe his tears and cut his mother's apron strings. I feel for the lad. He's such a big strong boy, but underneath that front, he's a sensitive lad. I've had my fair share of homesickness. I didn't realise how important it is to have people around you who understand your history. When it's not there, you have to explain yourself and you get sick of it, so you don't bother. Young Joe is going through that, I can tell. So I just listen. He seems to like that. I've become quite fond of him – like a little brother. And he looks out for me as well. He helped me cut down the bamboo. He cut. I stacked. He also took over most of the heavy work when we were ordered to build a latrine on top of a grassy rise at the back of the camp. He did most of the heavy digging of the hole exactly at the peak. I cut out the bottom of a drum that had been filled with flour, then mounted it over the hole Joe dug. The latrine doesn't have a roof or screens and is in full view of the camp.

There are two advantages. Occupants have a 360-degree view and lads below could see whether it was engaged, without walking up the hill. Pleased Horry, Tic and Sticks are here too. Good to have great mates.

Jock's diary shows his fascination with the local people and he wondered how they kept smiling through the constant rain and warring intruders. They waved and beamed betel-nut-red smiles whenever he saw them washing their clothes in the river or gathering water from further downstream.

One day Joe nearly drove him and Jock into a ditch when he came across a group of bare-chested women walking along the side of the road. 'Watch it, look where you're going, Forrester,' Jock said, grabbing the steering wheel just in time.

'Sorry mate.' Joe looked over and grinned. 'What a good telegram back home. Died on active service, looking at tits.'

Further along walked a native man carrying a spear and a small child. A few paces behind walked a tiny woman, naked from the waist up, who looked no older than fifteen. She carried a large woven bag suspended from a strap across her forehead and balanced on her shoulders. A mangy dog walked behind.

Laughter and squeals could be heard from the native boys jumping off the rocks into the river. A small child from a nearby village had been taken by a freshwater crocodile weeks before. But the youngsters weren't troubled. They climbed barefoot onto the rocks, grabbing the roots of the pandanus for safety. The vegetation grew out of a group of boulders and hung over the water's edge. The boys reminded Jock of shiny black seals as they played in the water. Flashes of white grins contrasted with their dark, slippery bodies ducking, weaving and jumping on one another.

Birds with plumage of brilliant blue, red and amber swooped among the trees. Jock had come face to face with a cassowary. It stood six foot high and had vibrant blue and red feathers on its face and neck, a brown helmet and yellow eyes that stared straight through him. After a few moments, unperturbed, it stepped back into the thick jungle. Jock had been on his way back from the river after learning the hard way about the green ants. He had swung his axe into the trunk of a palm tree dislodging thousands of insects. When they attached themselves to his bare back, he ran to the river and duck-dived in, boots and all. After that, there was an unwritten law in the camp, 'Don't disturb the ants and they won't disturb you.'[2]

Jock was expecting the order. While on night shift he had transcribed the command from headquarters to move into the jungle.

'Fall in line before dawn tomorrow. Full kit,' Broom yelled. 'Could be months, you miserable bastards.'

Jock packed small tins of bully beef, biscuits, rice, water bottle, blanket, grenades, gun, ammunition belts, notebook and HB pencil. The men's morale was heightened at the prospect of fighting a ground force enemy. The sixty-five airborne attacks in Darwin had left them beaten, ashamed of running, hiding, finding shelter and sleeping in slit trenches, learning to fear a full moon. During their eighteen months in the frontier town, the soldiers were sitting ducks. Now they were rested, fit, well-fed, familiar with the new equipment, and technically trained. They believed they were able to read maps of a harsh landscape, taught to use 24 x 25 pounder guns, with months of gun drill and mechanism courses under their belts. In addition to hardening up and technical training, they had spent time with their families. Jock had a fortnight with Bess and Cleary in Geelong, plus extended time with Bess while stationed in New South Wales. He was as ready as the rest of them. It was time to meet the Japanese on equal ground, face to face, gun to gun, bayonet to bayonet.

---

2 Jackson, R 1997, *The Broken Eighth, A History of the 2/14th Australian Field Regiment, Darwin – New Guinea – New Britain*, Clipper Press.

He wasn't prepared for the rugged and hostile terrain of New Guinea. None of them were. Water and mud dominated and Jock never got used to it. The rains came in the afternoon and continued until the next morning. He shivered through the cold nights. Water seeped into everything, wet clothes stuck to his skin and didn't dry, but fluctuated between soaked and damp. Jock remembered Bess soaking his singlets in the Rickett's blue bag water and saw the funny side of it. If she could just see me now, he thought, as he wiped his muddy hand across the front of his singlet. The once snow-white undergarment Bess was so proud of was beginning to rot and ponged from stale sweat and nights of lying in the mud.

A stubborn mass of forest covered the river's edge making it so impenetrable soldiers waded chest-deep into the water. In an attempt to keep his ammunition dry, Jock clipped his grenades higher onto his pack, slipped the belts of bullets around his neck and held his gun over his head. His arms and shoulders ached from holding them up for hours. The heaviness of the ammunition around the top of Jock's body added to the strain. Each step was taken carefully, not knowing whether water weeds, snakes or leeches touched his body. They were walking in freshwater crocodile territory and no-one spoke, in a feeble effort to be invisible. In time, they moved back to what they thought was dry ground but instead walked thigh-high into a swamp. The pong from the quagmire and rotting vegetation hit them with a force causing Jock to retch. Mosquitoes and insects swarmed around them, biting through clothes. Jock's face began to swell, welts covered his hands, arms and legs – itching like hell.

Day after day, the men walked without let-up. At dusk, Jock welcomed the sight of the blue and green fireflies, their pointless flittering heralding the relief of night. One evening, a scout reported swamp-like conditions continued for half a mile. Where they were was as good as any to try and rest.

The bog was now over Jock's ankles. He saw Joe, Horry and

Sticks attempting to make rough beds from branches and vegetation covered with a canvas sheet. Jock swung his pack off his back and hung it on a tree branch. Ninety pounds lighter was a relief. He placed his Owen in the fork of two branches to keep it dry, reclined against the tree and took turns resting each foot against its trunk. He removed his cigarette tin and matches from underneath his hat, lit his rollie then tilted his head against the tree, closed his eyes and drew on the fag. Horry sloshed up next to him. Jock passed him the cigarette and they stood there together, sharing the dank smoke.

'It's got atmosphere this place, hasn't it?' said Horry.

Jock opened his eyes and looked at the boy. All he could see of Horry's muddied and slime-covered face was his cheeky grin. His teeth were turning brown and black specks dotted his lower canines. Jock noticed his recently chipped front incisor. The boy winked with a bit of a nod. For a minute, Jock stared. They began to giggle. Horry's shoulders shook as they both tried to stifle their laughter, mindful it could alert the Japanese. Or worse, they'd be sent scouting up ahead with nothing more than their Owens and a couple of grenades as a punishment handed out by Broom.

Thick black clouds signalled another downpour. Jock knew it wouldn't be long before the heavens opened again. Within minutes, heavy raindrops smashed the cigarette and made a racket on the metal casing of the guns. Horry threw his canvas sheet over the both of them. Jock took one end and they stood there together huddled under the makeshift cover.

'Fuck a duck, what did I do to deserve this shit?' said Horry.

At the first rays of daylight, Jock opened a tin of bully beef and scooped out handfuls of the salty, fatty brown muck then wiped his hand on his singlet. He lifted his pack onto his shoulders and fell in line behind Joe and in front of Horry. The unit trudged on, squelching through the swamp until it petered out to thick mud. The narrow track snaked through dense jungle. The growth was so thick, Jock could only see Joe, Tic and Horry in front of him. He was pleased there'd been no order to carry a wireless and batteries into the jungle. A radio in such thick rainforest would be useless. Every step was precarious in the thick mud. The further they traipsed into the wilderness, the more they lost track of time and days. They stepped over or around fallen logs and rocks, pushing through the undergrowth. If they weren't slogging through mud, they were sliding on moss-covered fallen tree trunks, making it difficult to gain traction. Jock found it harder descending the hills than ascending, because of the pressure on his knees and ankles.

He sensed the foe close, on the ground, hidden in the bush, not in the sky as it was in Darwin. He imagined there were snipers everywhere. Even thought he could smell them. He remembered the musky odour of Japanese merchants he'd met in the dusty port town. Jock recalled stories describing the enemy's uniforms being designed to camouflage in the jungle – a stark contrast to the easy-to-see light brown outfits of the Australians.

They came upon an expanse scorched and smashed from an earlier conflict. The unforgiving landscape blackened from grenade and machine gunfire. Broken palm trees lay flattened on the ground and empty ammunition shells and missile cases littered the once pristine vegetation. The further they snaked into the wilds, the slower the progress – step followed hazardous step. Rain was relentless. After weeks of sleeping in slush, Jock's fingernails were embedded with dirt. It was in his pores, nostrils, eyes, and ears. The rain and malaria-carrying mosquitoes were his constant companions, large clumps of slush clung to his boots as he scrambled through the mud. Visibility was poor. Giant century-old trees all but snuffed out the sun, except for glimmers of daylight flashing through the tops of leaves and branches. Fog lingered throughout the day, making it hard to breathe. The nights were bitterly cold, and the sounds from the industrious nocturnal animals added to the fear. The trek through the snarled jungle was harsh, but Jock knew once they hit a clearing they were in worse danger and they needed to act fast. Run for cover first then assess the enemy's location before opening fire – all within a matter of seconds. While the tangled rainforest was hell, it had benefits. The dense vegetation hampered enemy fire.

'Jap camp beyond clearing up ahead,' came the word from Broom up front, each man whispering to the next.

Jock could see the panic in the boy's eyes when he relayed the message to Horry. 'We'll be right, mate,' Jock tried to reassure him. 'We'll be right.'

Another order came along the line. 'Stop at edge of clearing, bed down for night, attack enemy camp at first light.'

Jock kept walking, Horry was close behind, Tic and Joe followed. When they arrived at the spot where the unit had stopped, he took off his pack and stretched his neck and shoulders – relief from the weight. As light faded, he spread out in the wet undergrowth, resting on his elbows, keeping his tin hat and boots on and his gun close by. I'm so tired and old, he thought as he rested his forehead on his rolled up canvas sheet and closed his eyes. Let's hope the practice did us right.

Jock didn't sleep. He was on alert, listening to the night sounds. It was still dark when the men were woken in a domino effect, each man tapping the next. He folded his canvas and pushed it hard into his pack then lifted his kit onto his back, careful not to make any noise. At the first hint of daybreak, they crept towards the clearing through the last of the jungle, in the direction of the enemy camp to surprise them while they slept. Deep dread and fear twisted itself in the pit of Jock's stomach, the first stage of pure terror. His heart was thumping. His legs were sticks of jelly and he wasn't sure whether they'd hold him up.

'I'm shit scared,' whispered Horry.

'You're not on your Pat Malone,' Jock whispered back as he began to creep forward, each step slower and more deliberate. Jock's hands were sweaty, his breathing heavy, stomach tight. Tread lightly, he thought. He recognised the stench of rotting flesh – an old battlefield. Decomposing bodies from both sides merged with mud and trees.

A few yards to his right he heard a rustling sound coming from the edge of the clearing. On his left another sound from the trees. He tried to remember the drill: open space dangerous, stick to sides where there's cover.

A bullet whistled by Jock's ear. He dropped flat, clenched his teeth and lay still. A Japanese soldier, the size of a twelve-year-old, ran from the bushes, a submachine gun held hip-height. Thud! Thud! Thud! He was light on his feet and fast – so close Jock saw his squinting eyes. Jock's mouth was dry. He began to pant. Stay calm, he told himself. Stay calm. The enemy had taken two diggers and disappeared into the jungle before the Australians realised what hit them.

Jock knew then the enemy had been waiting for them. They were a step ahead. He remembered the training. If you walk into an ambush, shoot in the direction of the gunfire, then find cover. Joe and Horry were either side of Jock now. The three of them ran tossing hand grenades into the enemy hidden in camouflaged dugouts and under bushes. Jock was confused by the sudden chaos. Japanese armed with machetes, guns and hand grenades jumped out from the haze, yelling over deafening gunfire, and eerie smog hung in the air. Jock shot in the direction of the attack then he and Joe took cover behind a small hill covered with bushes. Horry kept running and shooting. 'Yellow Baastarrdssssss,' he yelled.

Jock saw Horry hit the ground. A grenade landed in the boy's path and he took the full force front-on, flew into the air and fell heavily. Jock crawled to where the youngster lay in the slush and his own blood. He stretched out next to him, his hands shaking as he pushed the boy's bloodied, shiny intestines back under what was left of Horry's shirt and held the lad to his chest.

'There, there mate. It's alright.'

The stench of entrails reminded Jock of pigs being slaughtered on the farms back home. The bony-boy ribcage moved in and out, the frail movement became less and less, until nothing, and then started again. Horry's eyes rolled back, he made a gurgling sound and spent his last minutes in the older man's arms, crying for his mother, oblivious to the din and madness around him. Jock leaned his cheek against the muddied and dented tin hat, not wanting to let go of the youngster. Such intimacy with a man was foreign in everyday life, but in the shithole of war, holding his young friend as he died was the most natural thing to do. Amidst the chaos of gunfire and grenades, Jock wept as he remembered the bull ant bites, the old man teasing and the young fella's bright eyes.

'God bless, son,' he said and pulled the canvas sheet they had both sheltered under weeks earlier, out of Horry's pack and covered him. Jock used his elbows and knees to lever himself along until he was behind a clump of trees to the side of the clearing. He stood and tossed three grenades in quick succession at the thicket from where the fatal missile had been flung. He waited until the enemy scattered then opened fire.

At night, exhausted men – enemy and friend – sat motionless, speechless. They used giant leaves as cover from the continuing rain. The medics did their best to attend to the wounded. This was the first combat for many. Mates were lost and maimed. Similar to Horry, many were left in the jungle to rot.

Jock collapsed onto a mossy log, his head resting in his hands. We're just ordinary men, he thought. This is hell. Fatigue swamped him. After weeks of being on full alert with little sleep, his body felt heavy as lead. Joe slumped on the ground next to him, lit a cigarette and handed it to Jock. 'Here mate, you could do with this.'

'I let him slip away, just a boy – did nowt.' He drew hard on the tobacco. 'Just left him to rot in the jungle, to be eaten by animals.'

'You were there, mate. He knew that.' Joe lit his own rollie.

'He won't know about them animals, but he knew you were there with him.'

'You're a good lad, Joe. Don't know I'd manage this hellhole without you,' Jock said as he pulled out his canvas sheet.

'You too, mate. You too.'

One by one, they crawled under their covers and rested while they could. Jock stuck a cigarette in each nostril, to keep out the stink of burning and rotting flesh. Same again tomorrow and the day after and the day after ...

How do these men from different sides of the globe, thrown together to slaughter and maim, forget? Their goodness plundered, turning moral men into murderers, their souls toxic from what they have done. How do they expel the poison filling their hearts and minds? How do they stop the noise in their heads, the bombing, the shooting, the yelling, the sobbing? They want to erase this chapter – but they can't.

No training had prepared Jock for brutal combat. Now the men had reached the enemy, their job was to push them back into the jungle until they retreated entirely or were dead. After months of stalking and fighting, the Japanese withdrew and the surviving Australians started the long walk back over the rough terrain to their base camp.

Jock trekked through the jungle, still on full alert, ready for enemy attack. The heat, oppressive humidity, hunger and lack of water added to his misery. He spoke to no-one. At night, as he tried to sleep in the slush and fend off the mosquitoes and leeches, he thought of Horry and was haunted by the last sounds the boy made.

In single file, they trudged through the unfamiliar jungle. Jock hoped the unit was headed back to Butibum and not forging further into the wilderness. It was weeks before he recognised familiar terrain. He crossed the river and the two mountain ranges came into sight. He followed the water until he saw the camp.

The sky was overcast. The tops of the Atzera were covered with thick mists. Breaks in the clouds cast shadows over the smaller mountain range. Light rain left surfaces damp and slippery underfoot. The men cheered feebly when they saw their base camp. They walked along the riverbank past clumps of bamboo where Joe had helped Jock cut the poles for the tents and where their friendship began. Jock remembered the cassowary and washing the green ants off his back.

Broom ordered them to fall in line.

Jock knew army protocol called for the commanding officer to ensure ammunition was cleared from guns after deployment. But thoughts of washing off the mud, slime, Horry's dried blood and sleeping in his own dry camp stretcher and not the wet jungle floor, consumed him. Caked in mud and looking as spent as his men, Broom stood in the middle of the clearing.

'Inspection of arms.'

Jock took his usual place in the second row beside Tic and Stan, with Joe and Sticks in front. He was mindful of the gap next to Sticks where Horry used to stand. One of many gaps left in the ranks.

Jock was finished. His legs could only just hold him.

On Broom's command, they removed the magazines of their mud-caked Owens.

On the next command, they opened the breech.

Jock noticed three foraging ravens taking off from the waste bins. The noise and quick movement of the drill startled them. They flew over the parade ground, squawking their annoyance at the interruption.

My father's diary ends after his return to camp. Medical records show his health deteriorated until his early discharge from the army in 1945. Military and medical records, war diaries and information sourced from veterans, helped me piece together the following chapters of his enlisted life.

Jock woke to the sounds of voices – women's voices. At first, he thought he was back in Clarence Street with Bess, her mother and sisters. Then he heard men talking and yelling and the motors of jeeps and trucks. He opened his eyes to a green mosquito net hanging six inches from his face and covering his entire body; through the net, he saw a high canvas ceiling. Two lines of thick bamboo poles held up the roof of the tent. The humidity and heat enveloped him. He was lying bare-chested on a high iron bed and wearing someone else's shorts.

He tried to get up – too heavy. His head was foggy. No other option but to rest his head on the pillow. He could smell antiseptic, mould and sweat. He thought of Horry, and then ...

Sadness and grief swamped him; his eyes filled. Why did I have to wake?

He hoisted himself up on both elbows, saw two lines of tall double bunks on either side of the tent. They were occupied by dirty and bloodied men with bandaged heads, legs, torsos or arms. A number looked in shock, with tremors. There were men similar to Jock, with no physical wounds. A few sat sideways on their beds, legs dangling over the side, blank eyes staring. So high were the beds that men sitting sideways on the bottom bunk couldn't touch the ground with their feet.

At one end of the long tent, he could see outside to the jungle. Soldiers were building huts in cleared areas. Someone shouted orders to the fuzzie-wuzzies,[3] telling them where to dig, place poles and flooring. A truck stopped. More shouting, the canvas flap was rolled back and secured. Soldiers carried more wounded past his bed. Jock wrestled with the netting. A nurse wearing a grey uniform and gumboots squelched her way towards him. Jock then noticed the floor – it was a bog.

---

3 Fuzzie-wuzzie was the term Australian soldiers called the New Guineans.

'No, no mate, you stay put,' she said as she came closer. 'You're not going anywhere.' Her voice was soft, with a strong Australian accent. He thought of Bess.

'I'm not wounded. Those blokes can have my bed.'

'You're wounded enough.' She tied the mosquito net into a ball above him. 'You stay there until we decide where you're to go.' She pulled a second pillow from the empty bed next to him and helped him sit up. 'Just rest, you've been through a bugger of a time. You don't have to do a thing at the moment.' She made sure he was comfortable, leaned on the side of the bed and patted his arm a couple of times. 'I'm Joan, I'm a nurse here.'

She had freckles on her face and arms, brown eyes and her straight brown hair was cut to just above her shoulders. When she smiled, her teeth protruded. It was pleasant and strange being so near a woman after being so long in the company of men. He stared.

'You're safe here, Jock,' she said and smiled. 'You're in the 2/9th Australian General Hospital, just outside Port Moresby. You were brought here after … well … you know.' As she spoke, she ran her fingers through her hair and poked it behind her ears. 'You've been sleeping a while, sedated, so I bet you think you've been hit by one of those trucks parked outside the tent. We've let the padre know you're awake. He'll be over soon.'

As she straightened the worn sheets on his bed it was as if she was talking to herself. 'Bloody Owens, you're not the first soldier I've nursed because of the faulty buggers. There's been a few. Had one bloke in here just the other week – he shot himself in the armpit during drill. The gun discharged when the butt hit the ground. 'Diggers' darling', they call them. Well, that's a joke if I've ever heard one. The 'diggers' devil', if you ask me.'

Jock continued to stare, realised his mouth was hanging open and snapped it shut.

'Are you hungry? You must be.' Joan patted Jock's arm again, straightened his pillow and tried to lift her feet out of the mud.

'The field bakery baked a batch of fresh bread this morning. I'll get you a slice or two before it gets mouldy. Happens quickly here in this humidity, either that or the rats get it. But you're in luck today, Jock. The Red Cross have sent over rations. I will see what I can rustle up.'

Jock watched as she squelched her way out of the tent.

Injured soldiers carried on canvas stretchers passed his bed. Many wounds were flyblown and putrid. The pong of rotting flesh hung in the air. One soldier's arms and legs were stiff and jerking as if he had an electric shock. He was semi-comatose and calling out. Jock counted another five with tremors.

Joan appeared again smiling. 'Your lucky day, mate.' On a wooden tray, she had a plate of bread and jam and a mug of steaming tea. Jock sat up, rested the tray on his lap and took a bite out of the bread. He closed his eyes and relished the delight of fresh bread and the sweetness of the strawberry jam. He ate hurriedly, licked the jam off his fingers, sipped his hot tea, placed the tray at the end of his bed, rested his head on the pillow and drifted off to sleep.

When he woke, a soldier with small crosses on each lapel of his shirt was standing by his bed.

'Hello Jock, I'm Father Pat Keane. Just came over to say gidday. Do that with the new boys.' The priest was clean-shaven, wet brown hair stuck to his head and his army shirt had dark, damp patches under the arms and across his chest. He brought over a high stool from the nurses' station and placed it next to Jock's bed.

'What can I do for you, Jock? A confession? A few decades then. I've got a spare rosary.'

Father Keane led the prayers. Jock closed his eyes, bent his head and prayed under his breath, moving his thumb and index finger along the beads.

A couple of years before my mother died, my brother recorded a series of conversations with her. She was ninety then and spoke

candidly of our father's breakdown, why it happened and life with
him after the war.

March 1945

Bess sat on the back seat of the bus with a string bag flopped on her lap. It contained two tins: one with Anzac biscuits she'd baked the day before; the other held photographs of their son and two men's handkerchiefs with the letter 'J' she had embroidered in navy cotton.

Her trip from Geelong to the Repatriation Hospital in Heidelberg took four hours on two trains, a tram and a bus. The last leg was the most trying – a bumpy bus ride along an unmade road past paddocks and a few houses scattered along the way. She was relieved when the bus stopped outside a cluster of multistorey red-brick and fibro buildings. Covered walkways surrounded a number of dwellings. People, cars and trucks provided the site with a sense of busyness. A high cyclone-wire fence around the perimeter reminded Bess of a prison.

She walked along a side street to the hospital's entrance thinking of the last time they had been together in Sydney, at Miss Walsh's house where they had rekindled their romance. She smiled to herself when she pictured the two of them squashed into that single bed. They walked together, hand in hand, back to the pine forest – predawn – the long kisses by the side of the woods before Jock left her to weave his way back to the barracks before sun-up.

'I wonder how it will be now?' she said to herself.

The hospital's entrance was just past St John's Theatre where a crowd of women milled on the footpath. A guard with a patch over his right eye sat in an enclosed booth at the gate's entrance. When it was Bess' turn to ask for directions, he pulled open the glass window, picked up a large hard-covered book alphabetised along the side, opened it at C, and told her to follow the yellow line on the duckboards until she reached Ward 15. 'You've got an hour.'

Bess walked along a dirt road around a large roundabout with a flagpole erected in its centre. An Australian flag flapped in the breeze. The covered walkway appeared to go on forever and created a wind tunnel. Bess shivered and wished she had worn her coat. Women and men dressed in army uniforms; nurses in full regalia and men in pyjamas and dressing-gowns moved around the grounds.

Metal tips on Bess' high heels clicked on the boards as she followed the yellow line. Women walked in front and behind her. No-one spoke. At times, a group filed off onto other duckboards. After walking for a time, Ward 15 came into view. She joined a group of women waiting by the entrance and reciprocated when a few nodded or smiled.

It wasn't long before a bell rang and the crowd moved through two glass doors. Bess walked towards a *Visitors Report Here* sign hanging over an enclosed cubicle. Behind the glass, a nurse sat at a desk writing in a large book. She wore a white starched veil and a pale blue short-sleeved uniform. Bess was taken by freckles on her arms and for a moment they looked familiar. She knocked on the glass and said, 'I'm looking for Jock Connor. Could you direct me to him?'

The nurse looked up and stared. Bess waited for her to respond, feeling uncomfortable at being watched. She asked again. This time louder, thinking the nurse may be hard of hearing, maybe she had been in the field herself.

'Is that you, Bessie Brown?' The nurse stood up, opened the door and came out of the cubicle. 'It is. It is you. I'm Joan Higgins from Balliang, your old neighbour. You used to drive my brother, Nugget and me to school in the jinker. Do you remember?'

The two friends hugged.

Her polished brown lace-ups squeaked on the linoleum floor and her starched uniform swished as she walked. Bess couldn't help thinking of little Joanie sitting on the jinker swinging her legs as they drove along the bumpy roads of Balliang. And here she was swishing through a hospital ward, looking very much at home.

Bess recognised the aroma of antiseptic and noticed blank beige walls. Vases of wilting flowers were a poor attempt to lighten the place up. A faded picture of King George VI looked on the weary and wounded. In places, the floorcovering curled up.

The two old friends passed bed after bed with men wrapped in bandages, and amputees with stumps swathed in tight white bandages. The ward was noisy from visitors and patients talking. Excitement filled the air. A few were out of bed and walked with their guests towards the gardens. Others were being wheeled in chairs or hobbled on crutches. It was a strange world for Bess, yet her old friend appeared in control. Joan stopped at the last bed.

Jock's eyes were closed, and Joan leaned over him and touched his arm gently. 'Jock, Jock, there is someone to see you,' she whispered. 'Someone, you will be pleased to see.' He was propped up in bed with pillows. A sheet and lemon hospital blanket were pulled up to his waist and tucked in on either side of the bed, accentuating his emaciated body.

A white singlet hung on his bony frame. His cheekbones protruded and his eyes had sunken back into his head. Bess moved little by little, shocked by what she saw. He opened his eyes. His once bright blue irises were now dull.

'Hello love,' she said and kissed him on his cheek. 'You're a sight for sore eyes.'

He looked at her, but there was no recognition. He looked at Joan and said, 'Who is it?'

'It's me, love, it's Bessie.'

'Who?'

'It's Bess. Bessie, your wife.'

He closed his eyes.

Joan indicated for Bess to sit on a timber chair between the window and bed. My mother remembered seeing a pine tree and bushes of purple and white agapanthus through that window. She closed the curtains in case the sunlight might disturb him, placed the tin of Anzacs on his side table and moved the glass of water closer to where it was easier for him to reach when he woke. She sat and watched his face, his thin, clouded, sad face and cried. It was his humour and sunny disposition that had attracted her. She remembered seeing him at the dances and the way he joked and smiled. In front of her now, he looked as if his light had been snuffed out. His bones poked through his flesh. Had he not eaten for months? She watched him sleep and this again took her back to the last time they were together at Miss Walsh's house in Sydney.

———

She had received his letter when he was stationed in New South Wales. The workers on the wharf had been on strike and the army was called in to load and unload shipments.

He had written …

> I'm just a train-ride away, pet. Why don't you come up on your own for a break for a while? I miss you and I need you. There is word we're to be shipped to New Guinea at any time and I don't know when I'll be back.

Bess knew she couldn't leave Cleary at home. Since the telegram announcing Frank's death, Mary's health had deteriorated, leaving her frail. Tilly and Honor had taken jobs in factories and were away during the day. She asked Dorothy if Cleary could stay with her.

'Of course Bess, go and spend time with your husband, the older girls can help out with Cleary.' Dorothy started to cry then and Bess put her arms around her.

'I'm so sorry, Dot. I shouldn't have asked.'

'Of course you should ask me. If I can't be with my Bert, then, at least, I can help my friend be with her husband. Stay as long as you can. Cleary loves it here with the other children and the two girls are a great help.'

Bess packed Cleary's clothes and his toys into a small case and walked to Dorothy's house holding her son's hand. She was torn. She didn't want to leave her little boy, but she did want to spend time with her husband. As they turned into the front gate, Cleary let go of his mother's hand and ran to the front door, calling, 'Ed, Ed.' Inside, she hugged him, kissed his cheek and said her goodbyes. Peggy took him outside and when he disappeared out the back door, tears welled in Bess' eyes.

Dorothy hugged her. 'Go, go and have a wonderful time with your husband and have an extra wonderful time for me.'

Bess had made herself a sandwich, a thermos of tea and said goodbye to her mother and sisters. She caught the train to Spencer Street and from there a train to Sydney. The trip took hours and she was pleased she had packed her knitting, a jumper for Cleary from unravelled wool, previously her cardigan before the moths found it.

Jock had written to disembark at the Holsworthy train station and included the address of a boarding house. The dwelling was red-brick with a high unkempt hedge for a front fence. Bess climbed the three steps to the front veranda and tapped the brass doorknocker. She waited then tried again. No answer. She walked around the corner and found a park with a seat. She sat and knitted a few more rows, and finished off the tea. It was late afternoon when she tried the house again – still no answer. She found a hotel and booked a room for the night. The following morning she walked to the house and tried again – silence. An older woman approached from across the road. Bess noticed how dainty she looked. She took small steps, waved at Bess and as she got closer said, 'I noticed you were here yesterday too, weren't you?'

When Bess explained her predicament, the older woman offered her rental of a spare room at her house, on the proviso she met Jock first. She said she didn't have much respect for soldiers. The room had a leadlight window overlooking red and pink rose bushes in the front garden. Under the window was a single iron bed with a patchwork quilt of burgundy and pink. The walls and ceiling were painted white and an oak wardrobe, dressing table and two comfortable chairs completed the picture.

Bess fell in love with it and an agreement was made.

'Ten shillings a week, including food; I have a vegetable garden and chooks out the back – everything is fresh. Now, I do need to meet Mr Connor.'

As Bess watched her husband in the bed in front of her, she smiled remembering how fond Miss Walsh had become of Jock. The older woman looked forward to his visits and made him scones and jam. He spent Sunday evenings with them and Miss Walsh cooked grilled chops with vegetables from her garden. When Bess returned to Victoria, Jock walked with Miss Walsh to church on Sunday mornings and stayed for lunch.

She was so grateful for her time in Sydney with her husband, even more so now. She remembered looking at him early in the mornings before sunrise. His face looked peaceful then. He slept with the corners of his mouth curved upwards. When he opened his eyes and saw her close by, his smile widened, 'Morning, pet,' he'd say. 'You're a sight for sore eyes.'

By her husband's bed at the hospital, Bess cried, using the two new handkerchiefs with the navy-blue 'J' embroidered in the corners. She held his hand.

'What's happened to you?' she whispered. 'Come back to me.'

The cafeteria was noisy with nurses, doctors and patients walking, talking and moving chairs in and out from tables on the hard floor.

Bess' eyes were red and swollen, her face and neck blotchy. She and Joan were silent as they stood in line for a cup of tea and piece of fruitcake. Bess followed her friend as they walked along the ramp and into the garden. Joan found a quiet spot with a timber picnic table and chairs set under a clump of pine trees. She placed the tray on the table and wiped the pine needles off the seat. The two women sat side by side drinking tea. Bess stared ahead. 'He didn't know me.' She placed her cup on the saucer then on the table in front of them. She picked it up again. 'He didn't recognise me.' She turned and looked at Joan. 'What's happened to him?'

'What do you know, Bess?'

'Very little; the army are stinkers,' Bess said as she rummaged in her handbag for one of her damp handkerchiefs and blew her nose. 'They said he had malaria.'

'He has been unwell.' Joan held Bess' hand. 'He's sedated at the moment and is coming right. Visit again. He will get to know you in time. You'll need to be patient.'

'What can you tell me? Anything, tell me anything. It will help.'

'I nursed Jock at the 2/9th Hospital in New Guinea,' Joan said, turning to face her friend. 'After that he was moved twenty-two times to different bases and hospitals across Australia and New Guinea.' She paused then and looked down at her lap. 'He was also here for a time, Bess.'

'He was here and the army didn't tell me.' Tears welled in Bess' eyes. 'Can the army do that, not tell me?'

'The army can do whatever it likes. And it does.'

The two women sat in silence. Magpies warbled and a slight breeze caused pine needles to float to the ground around them.

'Jock's been unwell for a time. That's why he was discharged.'

Bess slumped on the seat, head bent, twisting one of the sodden handkerchiefs between her fingers. She looked up at Joan. 'I received a letter telling me he was coming back to the Repat, but I wasn't allowed to meet the hospital ship at Port Melbourne. The letter said

I wasn't authorised to see him until I received another letter. That arrived yesterday. I came as soon as I could.' Bess turned to face her friend. 'Joanie, he didn't recognise me.' She dabbed her eyes.

'He will, Bess, he will. He'll get well again, just you wait and see.'

'His ribs and shoulders stick out.'

Joan watched her friend struggle with the news of her husband's prolonged illness. She didn't have the heart to tell her what she'd read in his records:

… this man appears too debilitated and rather too old for further service … Involved in an accident in NG … Upset by this. Married, one child … Court Martial charge still pending.

AFTER THE WAR

5 November 1945

THE KIDS IN THE street had been building it for days. Old fence posts, split palings, blown bike tyres, broken wooden boxes, couch cushions with stuffing and springs spewing out the sides, had been thrown in a heap on the spare block next to the dairy.

The first one in six years and everyone in the street was excited – adults as well as children. Life had been austere for too long. Grown-ups were looking forward to a reason to come together to laugh and share something other than sadness, grief and fear. Another signpost the war was over and everyday celebrations could be part of the regular rhythm of life.

Bess spent tuppence on a box of sparklers when she picked up her milk, bread and dripping from Mrs Mac's on the corner. As she left the grocer's, she bumped into Dorothy. 'Will I see you at the bonnie tonight, love?'

Bess nodded and smiled. 'The young bloke's looking forward to it – his first. So am I, I have to say.'

'Will your Jock be coming along?'

'Too right.'

'I'm pleased; I look forward to meeting him.' Dorothy smiled and made her way up the street.

Jock had not long returned from the hospital when he, Bess and Cleary moved back into a cottage in Anne Street. It was similar to the one they had lived in after they married. He had been welcomed home by the neighbourhood. Before he enlisted, he always had time for people and was interested in their lives. His witty one-liners and strong Lancashire accent and strange pronunciation of words intrigued them.

Not so now. He became irritated and offhand when people wanted to chat. Since his return, he kept indoors, sat in the lounge room smoking and staring. He knew he had to make a living for his family. The mill said his job was waiting for him, but he found it difficult to move back into the swing of life. Money saved from his earnings while he served was dwindling. Bess' part-time job housekeeping brought in a few shillings a week – rent money.

On cracker night, the three of them ate their tea together in the usual silence – corned beef, mashed potatoes and peas. Bess cleared the table, washed and dried the dishes, bathed Cleary and dressed him in his pyjamas, dressing-gown and slippers. She changed her clothes, brushed her hair, freshened up her lipstick and flicked lavender water over her face and clothes. There weren't many opportunities to dress up and she looked forward to the three of them going out together – the first since Jock's return. She stuffed the sparklers into her handbag and called out, 'I'm ready, love.'

Smoke wafted through the open flywire door. Chatter from families walking towards the spare block floated along the hall. Reg, Harry and Ed stopped at the front gate and yelled out for Cleary.

'He'll see you there,' Bess called back through the screen door.

Jock met her in the hallway wearing his singlet, trousers and slippers. A burned-down cigarette hung on his bottom lip.

'You and the boy go without me. I'll stay inside.'

'I thought we could do this as a family.'

'I said, not tonight, Bess,' he snapped, walked back to the lounge room and turned up the wireless.

It had been like this since he returned. Her husband was a ghost of the man she had known before he signed up. He was quick to anger and a different man from the happy, witty, loving person she had married.

He'll get over it, she told herself. Just takes time to adjust.

But he was different. When rats nested in the back shed, he waited in a dark corner with a piece of wood. Blocked all holes but one, and when the rodents scurried out he took to them with the four-by-two, bashing and swinging until they were more than dead. They were splattered against the walls, tools and stacked wooden crates. Night after night, he visited the shed until there was none left.

It's sport to him, Bess thought.

He'd go to bed late and wake a few hours later crying out and sweating, his chest heaving as if he were taking his last breath.

During the day, he was preoccupied and sat on the couch with a vacant look on his face. Bess thought he didn't want to be home and was reminded of stories she heard of other women's husbands who had cleared off weeks after their return to civilian life. And Margie, from the church, said her husband sat at the kitchen table and drank beer, from breakfast to bedtime. He had been in New Guinea too.

Bess closed the front door behind her and took Cleary's hand. They walked along the path and through the small front gate. The latch clunked. The aroma of burning wood and rubber became stronger the closer they got. The fire roared and crackled. Bits of debris flicked into the sky. The heat forced people to keep their distance. Bess' face flushed. When penny-bungers or double-bungers exploded or Katherine wheels lit up the sky, turning it pink, red and blue, people screamed and cheered. Cleary held her hand even tighter and sometimes wrapped his arms around her thighs. Dogs howled somewhere in the distance. Bess lit Cleary's sparkler then her own and stood with Dorothy and the children. She slipped her arm through Dotty's and whispered in her ear, 'He just didn't want to come. He's not the same, Dot, since he's returned. He's a stranger.'

Dorothy squeezed her friend's hand and said, 'It looks as if we've both lost our husbands in this blasted war.'

The children held their sparklers, mesmerised by the dancing flames in front of them. Before too long, the bonfire began to subside, and Cleary tried his hardest to stay awake. Bess could tell by his leaning on her and his constant yawning it was time for bed. He was nearly asleep on his feet. After bidding their farewells, mother and son walked back to the house.

Bess could hear the wireless as they came up the front path. She opened the flywire door, walked along the hall and took her son to the outside toilet. Back in Cleary's bedroom, she undid his dressing-gown and slipped it over his arms, pulled back the sheets and blanket and helped him climb into bed. His forehead was still warm when she kissed him and his hair smelled of smoke.

Crackers exploded up and down the street. A faint odour of gunpowder drifted through the open window. She turned out the light except for the child's rabbit night-light and pulled the door to, though left it ajar as was now the custom since Jock's return. Bess knew Cleary wasn't used to sleeping on his own.

She walked along the hall and opened the doors to the lounge room. The sound of an American big band blared on the radio. She walked to the sideboard and reduced the volume. Jock's feet and legs poked out from behind the couch. She pulled back the settee and found him on the floor, sobbing, rocking and holding a cushion over each ear. Bess sat on the floor next to him and waited until the noise of exploding crackers stopped before she removed the pillows. She lifted his head onto her lap and stroked his damp hair. They stayed on the floor in silence for what Bess thought an eternity.

In time, they sat silently on the couch together holding hands. She turned and looked at him. 'It's time you told me what's happened.' She paused, waiting for a response. 'I'm not leaving here until you do.'

They sat looking at one another. Neither of them spoke.

The familiar dreaded fear stuck in his gut, his chest tightened and tears formed behind his eyes. His breathing became deeper and he began to rock back and forth.

Through sobs, long silences and tears he told his wife the most painful and shameful of secrets …

Return from deployment – Lae 1943

Broom walked past lines of soldiers and inspected each man's gun. He stopped in front of Jock and ordered him to remove the magazine from his Owen. Broom checked to see no rounds of ammunition were left in the barrel. He continued the inspection until every man's gun had been checked. When finished, he walked to the front of the line-up and shouted, 'Weapons cleared. Dismissed.'

As Jock turned to walk back to his tent, he heard a loud, sharp, crack, a sudden pain pierced his ears and something warm covered his face. The barrel of his gun stank of gunpowder. He caught a whiff of the rusty, salty odour of fresh blood, burned flesh and singed hair. He wiped his cheeks and mouth, looked at his hand. Flesh and bone splinters covered his muddied fingers, gore splattered his shirt. He saw Joe Forrester fall forward, face first in the mud. The side of his head blasted, shattered as if an eggshell. Blood oozed from the gaping wound. The back of his neck and upper shoulders were covered with blood and bone fragments. His once strong shoulders, used to hoisting railway sleepers onto trucks and slashing bamboo stalks in one swoop were now lifeless, a palette of red, pink, grey and black. Blood seeped into the mud.

Everything slowed, as if Jock were in a slow-motion picture. What little strength he had, left his body, and he dropped to his knees; his thoughts ran into one another, jumbled words whirled around in his head. No. I've shot Joe. I've killed him. No, please God, please God, no. He opened his mouth to call Joe's name, but no sound came. In his mind he called: Joe, Joe, Broom cleared my gun. His mouth was open, but still no sound. He wanted to say, I'm coming, I'll help. He crawled on all fours to where his friend lay in the mud. Jock sat cross-legged and scooped him under his shoulders, pulled him against his chest, supported his head as if he were a newborn. Broom cleared my gun, Broom cleared my gun. Blood seeped through Jock's fingers and onto his shirt. Joe's eyes were closed, his breathing became deeper and faster, it decreased, stopped, started again. Breathe mate, breathe. Jock tried to say Joe's name, but still no voice. Seconds like minutes, minutes like hours. No going back. Jock was dizzy, his head pounded, he wanted to vomit.

Through the fog and noise, he heard men screaming and swearing, 'Get the fucking medics.'

Jock stared into Joe's face, nursing and rocking him back and forth, back and forth, come on son, come on, don't die, don't die. A faint voice became louder.

'Jock, Jock, can you hear me? It's time to let him go. We'll take him to the hospital.'

He looked across at a red-haired soldier no more than twenty, crouched beside him in the mud. A piece of white fabric with a red cross was tied around the top of his arm. Jock looked at his friend and loosened his hold.

'That's it, mate. We'll take him from here.'

Jock watched as Joe was placed on a stretcher, someone took his pulse another splashed disinfectant onto a towel and held it to the back of his head. Two men lifted him into the ambulance jeep and it sped away. Tic and Stan helped Jock up out of the mud and walked him around to the front of another vehicle and sat him between the driver and a medic.

'They're taking you to the hospital for a while, mate. Just until you settle.' said Tic. 'We'll come and see you soon, we'll come.'

Jock didn't answer. He sat in the middle of the two medics, eyes open wide, his face drained of blood.

Stan ran alongside the car as it accelerated, 'Me and Tic will come and see you soon, mate.'

Joe Forrester died on the way to the hospital.

I didn't take the opportunity or wasn't brave enough to ask my mother how it was for her knowing her husband had killed one of his own. I couldn't put her through such painful memories. My parents' aim would be to protect their children and not burden them with history – not consciously. And I imagine, in loyalty to my father, she would've remained silent or said, 'That was war; you'd either kill or be killed; you just got on with it; we didn't have time to navel gaze in those days.'

But this was different.

This wasn't the enemy. This was my father's friend; a twenty-two-year-old with the world in front of him. I can only envisage the anguish of thoughts and feelings she lived with. My mother's coping mechanism was to not dwell on things she couldn't change. I can hear her say, 'Just put it behind you, don't think of it.' On the recording with my brother, her pain was raw. She wept uncontrollably all these years after. I'm pleased my brother respected her heartache and did his best to help her through it.

Bess kept Jock's secret until she was an old woman in her nineties, but no doubt missed the man she fell in love with. There were a few brief moments, when he returned to his loving, funny, easy-to-be-with self – but perhaps those times were fleeting – before something triggered an angry outburst and then withdrawal. Bess could have consoled herself with the fact that he wasn't a violent man and he didn't drink or gamble – a good provider.

She heard other women talking of how different and difficult their husbands were on return from active duty. Many men had taken up drinking and lashed out verbally and physically at their wives and children. Violent arguments could be heard through thin walls, and wives sported black eyes and split swollen lips. Many men cleared off altogether, leaving families with no means of support.

The birth of Galvin and Rose in quick succession added to the pressure. Jock was offered a job at Yarra Falls Cotton Mill in Abbotsford on the outskirts of Melbourne, with better prospects and more income. His promotion meant moving away from Geelong, from Mary, Honor, Tilly, and Dorothy – Bess' support – to the outer suburbs of Melbourne.

'Perfect for a growing family,' he said as they walked through the front rooms of the house in Preston. They had taken out a mortgage. The house was sturdy enough, with sufficient bedrooms for a growing family. It needed a coat of paint and repair work.

'It's near schools, train, bus and tram, Catholic Church and there's a library on High Street, too, pet,' he said, smiling, searching Bess' face for a sign of enthusiasm.

He saw sadness.

The weatherboard dwelling was on an unmade road with potholed footpaths making pushing a pram strenuous. Paddocks surrounded the house and from the front veranda Bess could see a tannery, railway station and a red-brick Church of England. Out the back door the ground was flat and barren with patches of weeds, a young lemon tree next to the outside toilet and a dilapidated building at the end of the block. She couldn't help but compare life in this house to living in Anne Street where she could wheel the pram on paved footpaths to her mother and sisters' house or to Dorothy's for a cup of tea, where the children could play with their friends on soft buffalo grass and hide behind hydrangea and daisy bushes. Or she could walk along the foreshore to the beach and let the children run barefoot on the sand.

———————

Over a number of years, Jock's mother, siblings and families immigrated to Australia. They were part of the Assisted Passage Migration Scheme where adults paid ten pounds and children travelled free of charge. As each group arrived, Jock and Bess took their young family to Station Pier, Port Melbourne to welcome them.

It had been over two decades since his mother rolled over to face the wall the day he left England. But for Jock, the memory was as fresh as if it were yesterday. When he first saw Ada, he noticed how she had aged and shrunk. She was being assisted along the gangplank and lifted her walking stick just a small way off the ground and waved it back and forth when she first saw Jock. When she reached firm ground, he wrapped his arms around her and kissed her on the cheek. 'Mother, it's been a long time.'

'Yes, son and whose fault's that?' She looked up at him. 'And you've a strange accent.'

Bess kissed her on the cheek, welcoming her to Australia. 'And you do too,' she said to Bess, then busied herself with the luggage.

———————

Bess and Jock's house was near where his clan had settled. He found comfort with his extended family close by, and Bess delighted in seeing him relax and joke.

'War changes people,' she said when asked about the change in Jock.

My father had ten years with his mother before her heart gave way. I am not sure whether they made their peace. Both were damaged in their own way. For him, through the ravages of war; for her, I imagine, through living a tough life in England. During the last ten years of her life she lived in comfort with her children and grandchildren around her. Australia's warm climate eased the constant ache in her bones brought on from living in draughty old houses during England's bitter winters. This freedom from pain enabled her to move around more freely. She enjoyed going for short walks and playing cards with her grandchildren.

While it was still dark, Jock caught the train to Yarra Falls, returning early evening. On the weekends he planted trees and grass; built a sandpit between the outside toilet and back door; collected bits of old bicycles; made a couple of three-wheelers for the children and repaired broken weatherboards. Then Joseph and I were born. Now aged forty-four, Bess had five children to look after – four under six. They couldn't afford modern conveniences such as a washing machine or a vacuum cleaner and an automatic dishwasher seemed futuristic. The laundry was a lean-to outside, with two large concrete wash troughs. Attached to one was a metal clothes wringer with a side hand crank and two rollers for removing excess water from the wet laundry. Every morning she was first up. On hearing of Jock's painful farewell to his mother the morning he left England, she made a vow to herself she'd always be up to make him a cup of tea and breakfast before he left for work. She did this for all of us; she was always first in the kitchen boiling the kettle and making breakfast. She saw it as a personal failure if any of her family rose to a dark and empty kitchen.

Bess missed her mother and sisters even more now. She needed extra hands to help with looking after the children, shopping, cleaning and cooking. She often thought Geelong might as well be on the other side of the moon, instead of fifty miles away. She similarly missed her dear friend Dorothy.

I can't remember staying at the Grey Sisters, an order of Catholic nuns who offered live-in respite for mothers with young children. Mum stayed there with my three-year-old brother Joseph and me when I was under twelve months old. The home offered women a tranquil environment where they could rest while the nuns looked after their children. I don't know how long we stayed, but Mum spoke of our time at the Grey Sisters with great fondness. What a relief it must have been for her to have a place to rest and time to focus on herself while her two youngest were cared for by supportive, nurturing women.

It was around this time my brother Cleary joined the Marist Brothers in Mount Macedon. This wasn't to be his calling, and he returned home after the first bitter winter on the mountain.

My sister too spent time away from home. As a young girl, she stayed with my widowed aunt who lived a few streets away.

As the youngest, life whirled around me. I have no memory of any of these events, but the stories became part of our family folklore and indicated to me my mother needed help in the home.

Honor had been exchanging letters with Ralph while he was overseas on active duty. They were able to write what they found difficult to say face to face. He wrote from his hospital bed in Malaya telling her he had been wounded, leaving him unable to father children. On his return, they married, in secret, at the Geelong Registry Office, caught a train to Warrnambool and honeymooned by the beach. Ralph found it difficult to be around people on his return. When he wasn't working at his old job at the mill, he kept indoors too, just as Jock did.

Letter writing drew Bess and Honor even closer. Both their husbands were different after the war, and each sister was sympathetic to the other's experience. Tilly stayed in Clarence Street and looked after Mary's failing health. Dorothy remained single, never recovering from losing Bert. She continued working at the Ford factory and joined the tennis club. The children thrived and as they came of age found work in Geelong.

———————

Bess was ironing when the telegram boy arrived. She took the envelope remembering the last time she held a telegram. It had been when Frank was killed. This time, it was news of Mary.

> Mum in hospital. Severe stroke. Come quickly. Doctors don't know how long she has. Love Tilly and Honor.

The three sisters took turns sitting by their mother's bed. Bess found a bible in the drawer of the bedside table. She opened the dog-eared book at Ecclesiastes 12:6:

> *Remember Him before the silver cord is broken and the golden bowl is crushed, the pitcher by the well is shattered and the wheel at the cistern is crushed; then the dust will return to the earth as it was, and the spirit will return to God who gave it.*

Mary died later that night with Bess sitting by her bedside. She was buried with Tom in the Geelong Eastern Cemetery.

1962

Smokey, the cat, darted between my father's legs as he brought in a wooden crate from the shed. It was filled with briquettes and covered with a hessian bag to stop the black dust flying throughout the house. He wore his check work trousers, a grey shirt and burgundy cardigan. Green corduroy slippers – a Father's Day present from the year before – replaced his work shoes. Briquette dust smudged his cheek.

I was helping him light the fire by breaking up kindling and rolling newspaper into small balls. I placed them on the bottom of the grate with the twigs on top in a pyramid.

'That's an excellent job there, love,' he said, as he pulled a box of Redheads from his trouser pocket. He struck a match and lit edges of the crunched up Herald *under the kindling. The flames were slow at first, but the twigs caught alight within a couple of minutes. Dad placed a pile of briquettes and wood over the fire, making sure they didn't extinguish it, and rested one hand on the mantelpiece, watching to see if the flames were large enough to catch. The room was slow to heat, so I sat on the padded seat of the wood box next to the fireplace, tearing up strips of broadsheet. When they landed in the blaze, they ignited into tall dancing flames for just a minute or two then subsided. I threw another shred and watched it dance then wane, and another and another. I pulled out an old Footy Record from the box and tore it into strips. One section was too large and the page curled black on the sides, floated on top of the flames, then moved forward and nearly out of the fireplace. I picked up the poker and pushed the lit paper. I looked over at my father, not sure whether I'd be in trouble.*

'That was scary,' I said.

After a while, he said, 'Keep the bits quite small, love.' He stood up and walked over to where I sat. He knelt next to me and showed me the size by tearing up a piece of newspaper. 'No larger than that. If they're any bigger, they can float out and catch fire. You saw how that can happen.'

I tore up what was left, and threw sections into the blaze while, side by side, we stared into the fire. Eventually, Dad moved back onto the couch and Smokey curled up on his lap. The aroma of burning wood filled the room. My father looked peaceful. I wonder whether it was at these times he felt blessed, with a loving wife and five healthy children.

The fire began to wane, and I sensed my father's mellow mood. That's when I asked him the question. Was there something going on around me that took my young mind there? Possibly, I overheard a conversation earlier in the evening. It's hard to know.

'Dad, did you shoot anyone in the war?' I asked.

When he didn't answer, I looked across at him, unsure of the terrain again. He could explode for no reason. Not tonight, though. He was in a good mood and looked relaxed watching the flames. He said, 'Don't ever ask anyone who's been to war that question. They may have and don't want to talk of it.'

No angry outbursts on that day.

I felt he was trying to move close to me again after embarrassing me in front of my cousins the week before. We had visited their house and I was showing off by performing my new Irish dancing steps on the hardwood floor of their front veranda. My dance teacher, Mrs Connolly, had told me I must thump my feet hard – the harder, the better. 'I've seen competitions won or lost on the noise made from hard-soled shoes.'

I practised my steps whenever and wherever I could – in my bedroom, out on the concrete path behind the laundry and on the polished floorboards at school. Proud of the thunderous sound my feet made. I could tell the muscles in my calves and thighs were strengthening.

On that day, I had an audience with three of my cousins watching. I began by shuffling my feet quietly before building up to the loudest thuds on the hardwood floor. I focused all my strength on my legs and slammed my feet hard in a series of bangs.

At first, his shoulders twitched, then before I knew it he had whizzed around, grabbed me hard on the top of my arms, leaned over me and bellowed, 'Don't you ever do that again, do you hear?'

Jock picked up the worn, furry pillow from the cat's basket. He placed it under his arm and opened the back door so it wouldn't creak, just enough for him to slip through. He walked up the brick path, past the rotary clothesline and geranium bush, taking in the sweet blossom of the lone lemon tree in the garden. Not long up, the sun cast a mauve hue over the suburban backyard. Maggie, the magpie the children had named, perched on the high timber fence separating the family's house from the neighbours. The bird cocked her head then dive-bombed a worm. It struggled in her beak as she banged it against a rock. She flicked and flicked until it was lifeless, smashed, then she slid it down her throat and strutted on the dewy buffalo grass.

In the shed, Jock held the cushion between his knees; picked up newspapers from a bundle piled in the corner and spread them across the workbench. He placed the pillow on the broadsheets, pulled a ball of string and a pair of scissors out of his pocket and set them next to the cushion. A bottle of antiseptic sat on the shelf above.

Smokey had been ill for days, ever since Jock heard car tyres screech and the plaintive cry. Now the moggy's eyes wept, a viscous substance oozed from her nose and she hissed and whimpered when the children tried to pick her up. She was curled up on a stack of hessian bags at the back of the shed. 'You've made it easy for us, dear ol' girl,' Jock said as he picked her up gently, so as not to cause her more pain. 'It will be over soon. I should have done this days ago, shouldn't I, lovie?'

He placed her on the newspapers, stroking the parts of her body the speeding car hadn't damaged. 'Thanks for being a good friend,' Jock said. She looked up at him, her trusting yellow eyes dull and watery. She didn't struggle, as if resigned to her fate. Jock placed the pillow over her face and pressed hard. Her back legs jerked, but not for long. He wrapped her up in the newspapers then tied the parcel with string. Cat faeces and urine leaked through the newspaper onto the bench. Jock gagged and reached for the antiseptic. He tipped a big dash onto a flannelette rag. As he wiped the dark stain, the whiff of disinfectant brought back another time when death hung in the air.

He sat on a box and held his head in his hands. Two decades earlier when Jock was stationed in Lae, the aroma of disinfectant had filled his nostrils that day too. As they lifted Joe onto the stretcher, a medic tipped disinfectant onto the towel before placing it at the back of Joe's head.

'Jock, love,' Bess said shaking his shoulder. 'The children are up, they're looking for Smokey.' Jock was trembling and sweating. Still in her nightie, Bess took his face in her hands. 'It's not just the cat, is it, dear?' She placed her arms around his neck and held him. Her softness and scent broke the last of his defences. He sobbed into her shoulder. Husband and wife held hands, sitting on upturned tea chests in the dingy shed. The sun tried to poke through the filmy window in the far wall. The stink of Smokey's excrement mingled with the stale air. They heard the back flywire door open and twelve-year-old Joseph called, 'Ma-arm, Da-ad.'

Bess jumped to her feet. 'Come on, love. I'll make pancakes for breakfast. That will distract the little buggers. You finish what you're doing here.'

Jock placed the newspaper parcel on top of a pile of garden refuse in the incinerator, covered it with dry leaves then lit a fire. He put his hands into his pockets and rocked back and forth, watching the flames lick Smokey in the newspaper parcel, his mind hijacked by another time and another place.

As president of the local St Vincent de Paul Society, Jock took parcels of food and clothing to people and spent time talking with families, many the victims of drunk and violent men. His St Vincent's patch included Pentridge Prison, a bluestone jail built in 1850 to house the State's hardest and longest-serving prisoners. One Christmas Day, after the family attended Mass, opened presents and tucked into the celebratory lunch, a couple of men from the Society called around to collect Jock on their way to visit inmates at Pentridge.

———————————

Father Finbar Herrick's room was a five-minute walk from the main section of the prison and within earshot of the guard's voice over the loudspeaker.

The priest rocked back in his chair, cleaning his spectacles with a handkerchief. Dust motes hovered around his head, as the sun shone through an opened louvre window. The room was sparsely furnished, with two wooden chairs, a small table, a blue speckled ceramic electric jug, a few cups – a number with handles, more without – and a metal teapot covered with a yellow and red knitted tea-cosy.

Jock dropped onto the chair opposite Father Herrick. His shoulders slouched forward and his head hung low. He rubbed his ring finger across the middle of his forehead. His face was pale.

'How was Christmas morning at your house?' asked the priest.

'It's been the best of mornings and the worst of mornings. The children's squeals of delight woke me.' He looked up and half smiled. 'Such a joyful sound, Father – the best in the world. The boys got a cricket set and tin machine guns with batteries; when the trigger's pulled lights flash with a pretend machine-gun sound. They love them.'

Father Herrick inspected his glasses, put them on the end of his nose and said, 'I trust Santa brought your daughters something too.'

Jock took a deep breath and looked up. 'Umbrellas and toy pianos – which sound simple enough, until Joseph and Galvin took the umbrellas, climbed up onto the roof of the shed and jumped off expecting the opened umbrellas to break their fall similar to parachutes in war movies. They didn't. They turned inside out, snapping the frames, which got the girls upset and bawling. Galvin twisted his ankle when he landed. He was screaming in pain, and the girls stood around him laughing.'

Finbar chuckled. 'Was that the best or the worst?'

'Father, their joy was the best. The worst was this. A little while after the parachute incident, Joseph crept up behind Anne while she was teaching herself 'Three Blind Mice' on her new piano. I came in to see him putting the machine gun to her head and pulling the trigger. She wasn't having that; she spun around and punched him.'

'Good for her. What did you do? More to the point, how was it for you, Jock?'

'I grabbed the gun off Joseph and pushed him away. I don't know how hard I did it, but the look on his face said hard enough. I sensed danger as if it were life-threatening. As if Joseph was doing something terrible. But he was just being a pest of a brother, nothing more.' Jock rested his head in his hands then looked up at the priest. 'Father, I was terrified, speechless, sick, angry, guilty ... I was seeing myself and Joe Forrester. My heart raced ... The way he looked at me reminded me of when I grabbed Anne while she was showing her cousins her new Irish dancing steps, some weeks back. The fear and embarrassment on my little girl's face speared my chest.' He looked up at Finbar. 'You know she stopped her dance lessons after that. I frightened her so much.'

The priest looked over his glasses, watching his friend suffer. 'The past is the past; you can't change it, Jock. Jesus forgave sinners. It's time you forgave yourself.' He reached his hand across the table and rested it on Jock's forearm. 'It was an accident – a tragic accident. This is what happens in war. It wasn't your fault.'

Jock leaned back in the chair and closed his eyes. 'It doesn't matter how many times you tell me that, it was my gun, I was holding it, Joe's dead and I'm not.'

The priest walked over to the table and turned on the jug. 'Last time we spoke, we talked of what you might say to a mate who had experienced what you had. You said you were going to think of what you'd say. How's that gone?'

'I've tried to Father, but I've got no imagination. I try to conjure up a mate, but the only voice I hear is my mother's. It's not her voice; it's a sense of dread that comes over me that is connected with her. I can't even grab hold of what she is saying. But I'm left with a … with … hopelessness and I go into a fog. I can't think.'

Jock stopped talking and looked at the priest. 'Father, I can't even pretend I'm someone else.'

'Well, maybe that's not the way for you.' The priest poured hot water into the teapot. 'Cup of tea, Jock?'

'Yes, thanks, Father.'

As the priest placed the cup in front of Jock, he said, 'For Christ's sake call me Finbar or Fin, every once in a while, will you?'

'Righto Fin,' Jock said, looking up at his friend and making an attempt to smile.

The priest sat and stirred his tea. 'Was there any forgiveness or understanding of weakness when you were a lad in England?'

'Not that I can remember. My father was a hard man and he died when I was twelve. This made it difficult for Mother. She tried her best, but there wasn't any room for gentleness or forgiveness. We just knew life was tough and we had to be tough to survive. Everyone did. It wasn't just us.'

'Yet Jock, you sit and listen with great compassion to brutal men and murderers. Many have killed a number of times. I've seen you listen and talk to them without judgement. They open up to you. You make them smile and laugh. You treat them as equals. Don't you deserve not to be judged, too?'

'But Father, they don't know who I am – what I've done. And besides, now that you mention it, I am equal to them. I took a life. Doesn't that make me a criminal too?'

'No, it doesn't.' Finbar stopped stirring his tea and placed the spoon on the saucer. 'You are a good man who joined the war effort for his country and was involved in a tragic accident.' He stopped talking, lost in thought. After a time, he looked at Jock and said, 'Or did you intend to kill your friend?'

'Hell no, Father, I mean Fin.' Jock got up and walked across the room. 'What sort of mongrel do you think I am? Of course I didn't shoot him on purpose. It was an accident. That blasted Owen misfired. It was supposed to be empty. Broom checked my gun and gave me the okay.' Jock flopped back onto the chair and rested his chin on both hands. 'I've replayed it so many times. If only I could take it back. I hate myself.'

'But you can't take it back. Let that idea go. What you can do is forgive yourself now. Just try forgiving yourself a small bit. It doesn't have to be for the whole accident. Forgive yourself for as much or as little as you can right now. Jesus forgives you. Do you think you know better than Him?'

Jock looked up at the priest and nodded his head. 'When I hear you say these things in our meetings, Fin, it makes sense; but in the day-to-day business of living, the darkness returns.'

The two men sat in silence until the voice on the overhead speaker announced visiting hours would begin in fifteen minutes.

'How about absolution again?'

Jock shrugged, but he knelt, clasped his hands in front of his chest and bent his head. Fin rose, pulled out the folded purple stole with gold edging from his back pocket. He kissed it, placed it around his neck and stood in front of Jock. He rested both hands on his friend's head before making the sign of the cross.

Pater misericordiárum, qui per mortem et resurrectionem Filii tui, et in Spiritu Sancto et mundum reconcilians tibi in remissiónem peccatorum. Per ministerium Ecclesiae indulgentiam Deus det tibi pacem. Ego te absolvo a peccatis tuis in nomine Patris et Filii et

Spiritus Sancti. Amen.
God the Father of mercies, through the death and resurrection of
your son, you have reconciled the world to yourself and sent the
Holy Spirit among us for the forgiveness of sins. Through the
ministry of the church, may God grant you pardon and peace. And
I absolve you of your sins, in the name of the Father, and of the Son
and of the Holy Spirit. Amen.

Jock said 'Amen' with the priest and made the sign of the cross. 'Thank you, Father.'

Finbar helped him up. 'God bless, son. Let's go; visiting hours started five minutes ago.'

When Jock returned home hours later, Bess met him in the kitchen still wearing her best frock, the one she kept for special times as on Christmas Day or the odd occasion they went out. She had long kicked off her shoes and her bare feet made a soft padding sound on the linoleum. Delicate tendrils from her pinned-up hair escaped down the back of her neck.

I peeked through the crack where the sliding door hadn't closed against the doorjamb.

'Your place is at home with your family on Christmas Day,' she said in a hushed voice, thinking no-one could hear, but I saw and heard everything.

Jock opened a kitchen cupboard door and put two mugs on the bench.

'But Bess, these blokes have no-one. But for the grace of God, love.'

'I know what that means for you, but not Christmas Day, that's all.' She walked over to the kitchen sink, turned on the tap and filled the kettle. 'The kids wanted you here. I wanted you here. The boys got a new cricket set for Christmas and they wanted you to play a game with them.' She placed the filled kettle on the stove and lit the gas jet. 'They're very disappointed. Not Christmas Day, other days, but not today.' She walked to the fridge and picked up a bottle of milk, then poured small amounts into the mugs. 'It is not too much to ask. You didn't have to visit prisoners today. Your family is more important than strangers.'

'Alright, Bess.' Jock was getting agitated. He poured the hot water into the teapot, swirled it around harder than usual and placed it with a thud on the kitchen bench.

Bess stopped talking.

He waited a few minutes then poured out the steaming tea and took the two mugs over to the kitchen table and sat. 'I'll ask the blokes without families to visit next year.'

A Christmas cake covered with a net food protector sat in the middle of the table. Bess cut two slices and placed them on a small plate.

'We'd be happier if you did that. Your family comes before strangers.'

'I hear you, don't go on.'

'I was just saying.'

They sat together in silence, drinking tea and eating Christmas cake.

At times, the controlling, angry father was absent and he enjoyed watching his children's antics. I remember the times we rode on Melbourne's old red rattler trains to Flinders Street. He often took the three youngest, Rose, Joseph and me to the football on the train, leaving my mother time to rest. The two older boys were grown-up enough to go off on their own.

On the way to the railway station, we'd race one another to what had now become a busy crossroad at the end of our street and wait on the edge of the footpath. The traffic controlling device was a tall tower with a large circular disk on top. It reminded me of a clock, but instead of numbers, there were sections of red, green and amber. A moving hand in the middle of the dial indicated who had the right of way, and how long they had left. Even when the moving arm had landed on green, indicating it was safe for pedestrians to walk, we'd remain on the footpath until Dad clapped his hands twice. We knew the drill. He often used this clapping of hands as a form of direction for us: if he wanted us to return to him, as well as when to walk across the road. This wasn't out of the ordinary for us when we were young. But on reflection, it was a ridiculous way of communicating with children. As I moved into adolescence, I dreaded his clapping in public and even ignored it at times. In time, it stopped. I don't know why or when.

On the way to the train station we walked past the old smelly tannery, the last in a number of similar factories built in the shire in the late 1800s. The calfskins arrived at the mill stiff and dirty, caked in blood and gore. If the wind blew a particular way, the pong of rotting flesh wafted up to our house. Hot days with a northerly wind were the worst. Windows and doors were kept closed. My father was often withdrawn on these days and it was best to keep out of his way. I wonder whether the odour of decaying meat could have triggered memories of the stink of death in Darwin and Lae.

Everyone was pleased when the processing plant was demolished and replaced with a petrol station, shopping centre and large car park. Across the road was a timber mill and next to that a vast stretch of vacant land with a dilapidated fence made from sheets of corrugated iron nailed to wooden posts. This became the site of the now bustling Preston Market.

As we waited on the station platform, we vied for a train compartment to ourselves in an old boxed-carriage red train. This meant we could use Victorian Rail as a playground. I remember my father being relaxed on these train trips. Under his watchful gaze, we slipped into a world with fewer rules. Maybe, moving from one place to another took him back to the new-found freedom he first experienced in shipboard life. Eight weeks on a ship on his own, not being accountable to anyone, must have been such a relief to him. He only had himself to please. He could do whatever he wanted when he wanted for the first time in his life. He too had the added luxury of a warm place to sleep and plenty of food. In this liminal space on the train travelling between home and Flinders Street, I wonder whether the freedom experienced on the ship resonated within him and he relaxed.

My siblings and I made the most of this carefree father as we travelled into the city. In each train compartment, two lines of leather handles hung from the ceiling. They were for commuters to hold on to when the seats had been taken. For us, these were perfect for swinging from handle to handle to see who could make it first to the other side of the carriage. I was the youngest, smallest and weakest and always last in the swing-on-the-handle race, or I lost my grip and fell onto the grimy floor littered with discarded chewing gum, spilled drink and ground-in food. My favourite pastime on the train was to stick my legs out the window. Opening a window on these old trains was difficult for many adults, near impossible for a youngster. There was a lever on either side of the top of the window. Dad stood at his full five foot ten inches and pulled both handles inwards at the same time. He released the window in one movement, so it slipped into the wall cavity. The timber-framed glass panels rattling within the hollow space helped christen these trains – the red rattlers.

I tucked my socks into my shoes and placed them under the seat. Then I'd sit sideways on the green leather seats, shimmy over on my bottom so I was pressed hard against the wall cavity and stick my legs out the open window. The cool breeze on my bare legs and feet was freedom. It didn't matter how brisk the weather. This was a time of breaking rules and a burst of fresh winter air wasn't going to dampen the fun. When the train whizzed by a steel pole or tree, I pulled my legs in as I thought my feet would be squashed.

It was thrilling and I laughed and squealed with delight, kicking my naked legs in the breeze. At times, Dad lowered whatever he was reading, leaned his head against the headrest and smiled, amused. Other times, he sat reading his newspaper or the Readers' Digest. When the train approached a station, Dad said without lifting his eyes, 'Station coming up.' We assumed the position of good children sitting on a train, hoping like hell that no-one spoilt the day's gymnastics by entering our compartment. When the train slid out of each station, we resumed our antics.

If we caught a new blue train, the stakes got higher. These trains weren't limited to tiny compartments; they were open plan and had numerous handrails to swing from. It was tremendous fun. If passengers boarded, we knew what to do. We sat like model youngsters, smiled and talked to one another, or sat and stared out the window. My father nodded to people and often started up a conversation or read The Sun newspaper from cover to cover before starting the crossword. Strangers on the train often commented to our father about his well-behaved children.

I could tell this made him proud.

At Flinders Street, we walked to St Francis' Church in Lonsdale Street where we attended Mass or confession or both.

I loved entering the side altar and lighting a candle. This altar was a magical place and I often spoke to God after dropping my sixpence into the metal honesty box. When my candle was lit, I'd walk to the back of a line of pews and sit on my own. I was confident I was the chosen one. God was all ears now, whereas other times my pleas to Him were ignored. Like the time I prayed very hard for a baby sparrow to survive. It didn't. I had found it in the doorway of a shop in High Street on my way home from school. Its mother was close by and I knew I should have left it. But my schoolgirl-self was compelled to pick up the fluffy chick and carry it home cupped in both hands. Even though I supplied the fledgling with worms from the garden and made it a nest out of twigs and strands of wool from Mum's knitting basket, it was dead in the morning. I buried it under the lemon tree in the back garden and made a cross out of two icy pole sticks I had found in the rubbish bin.

Then there was the time I prayed to be given a pony. My litanies weren't answered then either.

My father often stayed in the central part of the church after Mass had finished. He'd kneel, place both elbows on the back of the seat in front of him and rest his forehead on the top of his clasped hands. When he looked up, he had a red mark on his brow. We knew not to interrupt him unless it was urgent. When the time came, he'd gather us up from the side altar, where by now we were bored and hungry and sometimes hovering around the candles, blowing them out and lighting them again. Once, I picked up the honesty box chained to the top of a long, heavy candle-holder and noticed dents around the padlock and the slit on top. I turned it upside down and tried to shake out a few coins, but it made too much noise so I placed it back as quietly as I could.

My father appeared peaceful after these church visits and cracked jokes, making us laugh on our way to the next stop – to buy lunch.

There was a shop in Swanston Street with a state-of-the-art doughnut-making machine. I'd press my face against the glass panel and watch a silver arm drop blobs of dough into boiling oil. When the pale yellow circles turned to golden brown, another mechanical arm flipped them into a tray of sugar and cinnamon. At the end of the machine a man in a white coat buttoned on one side used tongs to place them into brown paper bags ready for sale, leaving the top open so the steam could escape. Watching the cooking method was hypnotic. I liked to pick out a particular one as it dropped into the hot oil and watch its journey until it landed in the paper container. I wanted my father to buy the bag with my particular doughnut in it. This didn't happen as there were people *in line before us who scored the one I had dibs on. Dad bought four doughnuts and four Four'n Twenty pies in separate brown paper bags. Each had a picture of black birds flying out of the top of an open red pie. This too was a treat, your own pie in your own paper bag.*

At home, we didn't get a pie each, Mum bought a family-sized meat pie and cut it into triangles. To make the meal stretch to feed seven, she boiled up a big pot of potatoes then mashed them into oblivion with a fork, slopped in leftover cream and a big dollop of butter. I liked to plop extra butter onto the creamy white mound and watch it melt and trickle down the sides.

With our hot pies and doughnuts, we walked to the Yarra River, sat on the grass and ate our lunch. When we had our fill, we shook our paper bags upside down. This sent flocks of scavenging seagulls into a frenzy as they dive-bombed and fought one another for the scraps. Years later whenever I walked past that spot by the Yarra, I could taste those Four'n Twenty pies.

It was a thirty-minute walk to the Melbourne Cricket Ground. Rose, Joseph and I ran along the Yarra, throwing stones into the water or racing one another to the next tree or seat. My father strolled behind deep in thought.

One day, when the football ground came into view, I said, 'Dad, can I buy a Footy Record? It's my turn.'

The Football Record was a mandatory accessory when watching a game of Australian Rules Football. It contained the latest news on the players and a section where you could keep track of the goals and points scored.

'Too right,' he said. 'But not now.'

I held his hand and we walked among the elm trees past big boys selling the programs in the best positions near the railway station. Rose and Joseph ran ahead throwing piles of dried leaves at one another. In the distance stood a skinny boy who looked to be around ten, with a canvas bag overflowing with Records. It was obvious his sales were small. By the time the football crowd had reached him they had bought their books.

'Buy it from him,' Dad said as he handed me a two-shilling piece and pointed to the kid. I went up to the boy, he took the money and smiled. I noticed his decayed teeth. He handed me the change and a Football Record; I passed both to my father. Dad did something then I hadn't seen him do before. He handed the change back to the boy.

'There you go, son.'

My father shoved the book into his back pocket and we walked together hand in hand. Out of the blue, he said, 'Those big brutes take all the good spots.'

'What brutes?' I asked.

'Those ones close to the railway station. It's not fair that little lad misses out.'

As we moved closer to the football stadium, I saw Rose and Joseph standing by the turnstiles, and asked, 'Dad, can I hold the Footy Record?'

As he whipped it out of his back pocket and passed it to me, he said, 'We'll keep it, and use it to start the fire sometime.'

Jock often reached out to the disenfranchised at other times, too. The day after the football match, he brought home a dinner guest, Roy Reeney, to share the family's traditional Sunday roast and watch television with us. Mr Reeney was a member of the St Vincent de Paul Society. A short, rotund man he lived in a boarding house near the church. He had a crimson complexion, thin greasy hair, a turned-up nose and little piggy eyes. He wore slippers and smelly socks. He laughed and made corny jokes while we ate our roast lamb and vegetables. We hadn't met anyone like him and we were fascinated – for a while.

After dinner, everyone moved into the lounge room to watch the Sunday night TV shows: *Disneyland* and *Father Knows Best*. As the evening progressed, the stink from Roy's feet made us ill, and we tried to hold our noses and breathe through our mouths. Rose left the room and soaked her handkerchief in Tabu perfume. She took a big sniff then handed it over and I did the same and passed it back. We took turns passing the scent-soaked handkerchief between the two of us until the heavy fragrance overpowered me, leaving me with a headache. One by one, we slipped off to bed. By the end of the night, it was just Jock and his guest left watching television. The following day, we grumbled about Roy's smelly feet and Jock responded by telling us we were selfish and uncharitable. Bess agreed with us, but she left the complaining to her children.

Roy wasn't invited back again.

Another time Jock offered a leg-up to one of his St Vincent de Paul's colleagues was when he invited Mr Comervich to paint the laundry and toilet. Jock's friend had six children, was a mechanic and a handyman of sorts, but found it difficult to keep a job. Mr Comervich had a speech impediment caused by being born with a hole in the roof of his mouth. At first meeting, he was difficult to understand, but in time your ear became familiar with his speech and conversing with him wasn't difficult. He reminded me of someone who had fallen into a ragbag and came out wearing whatever clothes had stuck to him. Mr Comervich was one of those people who had the ability to sail through criticisms and jokes at his expense. It was as if life's slings and arrows didn't touch him. He lived with much ridicule yet always had a sunny disposition and was kind and loyal to Jock, driving him where he wanted to go. In Jock's ailing months he was a regular visitor. He told him the latest news or just sat in silence with him. His eldest daughter Janine was in my class at primary school. She had the sharpest mind, always came top of the class and was the first to ask a well-thought-out question. She too was kind, had many friends and oozed confidence. I heard later she studied medicine at the University of Melbourne.

Mr Comervich was earnest in the task and painted everything in front of him. Instead of moving an old umbrella left hanging behind the laundry door, he painted around it, leaving an umbrella-shaped-silhouette. An empty, washed jam jar left on the laundry windowsill was painted, but underneath wasn't.

On one of the days Mr Comervich was working at our house, Bess had bought a jam sponge roll from the local cake shop for morning tea. She cut a few slices and left a large piece uncut. When she offered the cake plate to Mr Comervich, he picked up the large uncut section and took a bite out of it. Jock, Bess and I sat in silence drinking our tea and eating dainty slices of cake.

He regularly left his calling card in various guises. Once, he used one of our timber dining chairs as a sawhorse. He sawed right through its seat, taking a decent piece off its corner.

I was beyond proud the day I captained our school's criss-cross team to victory at the sports' carnival. After the winner's presentation, I ran to my parents watching in the crowd with my blue ribbon with gold 'First', pinned to my sports' tunic. Mum did her best to smile, but my father's expression was blank. I couldn't fathom the look on his face. It appeared I'd disappointed or annoyed him.

Yet I had won.

There was no enthusiasm, no celebration from either of my parents.

'The starter gun is too loud, it's giving me a headache,' he said. 'We're leaving.' He pushed a coin into my hand. 'Buy yourself an ice-cream on the way home.' Then my parents turned and walked away leaving me alone in the crowd surrounded by other kids' parents who were making a fuss of their children who hadn't come anywhere near first.

His dark mood remained during the evening.

My uncle, aunt and two of their friends visited. We weren't expecting them. They were in the neighbourhood so thought they'd pop in. Mum was pleased to see them and ushered the group into the kitchen. She pushed her hair back behind her ears and took off her apron. She left the room to change from her slippers into her day shoes and apply a smidge of lipstick.

Back in the kitchen, Mum picked up the kettle and began to fill it at the sink. 'Cup of tea, anyone?' she asked.

'Too right,' my aunt replied.

Mum made an attempt to tidy the kitchen as best she could while boiling water and placing cups and saucers on the kitchen table. She wiped crumbs off the benches and told my sister and me to move the newspapers off the kitchen chairs so the guests could sit. She reached up and took one of her best plates from the top cupboard and opened a packet of Chocolate Royals. My father and the guests sat around the kitchen table. My brothers, sister and I hovered behind the chairs waiting to pounce on the chocolate-covered biscuits when it was our turn. One of the guests – a stranger to us – pulled out a small packet of Craven As from his suit-coat pocket. He tapped the bottom of the soft pack on the table and three cigarettes popped up. He placed his lips on the tip of the highest cigarette then drew it out of the pack. From another pocket, he pulled out a silver cigarette lighter and flicked his thumb over its top causing it to flip open. He flicked his thumb again and a tall dancing flame appeared.

My father leaned forward so his face was inches from the guest. He looked him in the eye and said, 'No smoking in the kitchen. If you want to smoke, go outside.'

Everyone stopped talking and stared at the cigarette hanging in the man's mouth. My father was straight-faced and his delivery firm. There was no saying no to him. His word was law in his home. The visitor took the cigarette out of his mouth, placed it back in the soft pack and slipped the Craven As into his pocket.

Uncomfortable silence hung in the air until my mother walked over to the table. Her shoes made a squeaking sound on the linoleum. She set the plate of biscuits in the middle of the table, put her hand on my father's shoulder, smiled and said, 'Chocolate Royal anyone?'

Later that night, Mum visited my bedroom. 'I've just come to say goodnight, love.' She sat on the side of my bed, stroked my hair, picked up my blue 'First' ribbon from my side table and rubbed it between her fingers. 'It's nice and shiny. How are you after your big win today?'

'Good,' I said. But inside I wanted to cry and didn't know why. 'Good,' I said again.

'You did well, love, I was proud of you today. God bless.' Mum kissed my forehead. She walked over to the door and placed her hand on the light switch. She turned, looked at me as if she wanted to say something, waited a while, then said. 'Night love.' She flicked the switch and the room turned dark. I reached for my ribbon on the side table and slipped it under my pillow.

Jock's war scars weren't always evident to the family. He often played the clown and tap-danced in the kitchen with a funny look on his face. Or he played the 'bones', a musical instrument similar to playing the spoons – an Irish tradition. Except, he used animal bones dyed black; each one was approximately four to six inches long. He had two pairs and he'd hold a bone either side of his middle fingers and move both hands in circles, knocking them together and making a clacking sound.

His dry sense of humour made us laugh. While he was the master of his own house and a disciplinarian, there were times when he was kind and gentle. He had unfathomable patience when helping me with long division at the kitchen table until I was so tired he'd tell me in a soft voice, 'Time for bed. We'll try again tomorrow night.'

As a young child, I had bouts of tonsillitis and a series of abscesses in both eardrums. When ill, it was Dad I wanted. He was the tonic.

When pain interfered with my sleep, he rocked me in his arms singing in a low voice, Bing Crosby's version of 'Beautiful Dreamer'.
But I didn't remember this for years.

One spring day, I was showing my ten-year-old daughter how to bake a cake. I thought it an excellent opportunity to listen to a new CD of Roy Orbison's greatest hits. Perfect background music while mother and daughter baked together. Knowing most of the words to the more well-known songs, 'Pretty Woman', 'Crying', 'She Wears My Ring', I sang along while I showed my budding cook how to crack eggs without dropping shells into the mixture, and how to measure the sugar, flour and milk.

My daughter was greasing the cake tin while I creamed the butter and sugar when the first few bars of the next track came on. I stopped whisking. It must have been over thirty years since I'd heard 'Beautiful Dreamer'. Then Orbison began the lyrics, his melancholic voice gracing them with the emotion they deserved. Transported back to being rocked in my father's arms I dropped onto the kitchen chair and sobbed. The sense of grief and heartbreak consumed me. Why such an emotional charge? Was my response to hearing 'Beautiful Dreamer' nurtured by my father's own emotional charge when he sang this song to me – not another melody or lullaby? Was I his beautiful dreamer? How was it for him to see his baby girl so ill and in pain and not be able to do something to ease her suffering? Did this bring up memories of when he couldn't help others he cared for? Bridget? Horry? Joe?

My daughter was shocked. She walked over to me, carrying the half-greased cake tin. When I tried to explain to her what this song meant to me, she began to cry. 'It's not fair. I didn't get to meet my grandfather.'

That night, I couldn't sleep with the tune of 'Beautiful Dreamer' playing in my head and the emotions of the day swirling around my body. A tsunami of tears sat behind my eyes; my stomach

had that dull nausea I've come to know as a sign of grief. I tiptoed
to the kitchen to make myself a Milo and wished my father was
still alive, so I could have had an adult conversation with him.
So I could tell him what my research had turned up. I played the
chat in my mind. If he had been alive I imagine our conversation
would have gone like this.

The kitchen light was on and Dad was sitting at the table nursing a
mug of tea. He looked lost in thought. I wasn't sure whether I was
intruding. 'How about a bit of company, Dad?' I said, closing the
sliding door behind me, making sure it didn't thud.

'Yes pet, come in. What are you doing up so late?'

'I could ask you the same.'

'Have trouble sleeping these days. Thoughts take hold.'

'A penny for them?' I asked. He smiled. I moved quietly around
the kitchen, as being awake in the middle of night dictates. One
part of me was measuring Milo and warming milk in the saucepan.
Another was assessing my father's mood. A habit learned long ago.
But this night, he appeared relaxed and open. I wasn't sure whether
it was tiredness or that magical time of night when people's defences
haven't yet stood to full attention.

Here goes, I thought. 'Dad, can I ask you something?'

'Depends what it is.'

'It's about your time in the war.'

'Maybe not, then.'

'It must have been terrible. I'm interested to know how it was
for you.'

'How was what for me?'

'Dad, you know what I mean. When your gun discharged
shooting Joe Forrester?' He looked up, surprised. His jaw dropped,
causing a small gap to show between his lips.

'What do you know of Joe Forrester?'

'I'm a writer, Dad. I research things. It's part of my job.'

'Why do you want to know? It's a long time ago. Better leave the past alone.'

'Because it's part of you and I'm part of you, so it's part of me too in a way.'

'I hope not, pet. I don't want you knowing anything about that. It's a scourge, and I've done my best to try and forget it. Why do you want me to dredge it up again?'

'I don't want to cause you pain, Dad. That's the last thing I want. I thought it might help to speak about it, to share it with someone. Someone who loves you, who thinks you're the bee's knees and won't judge you. You're marvellous the way you've been able to live a respectful and rich life. Many couldn't, you know that. Many didn't.'

'What do you mean?'

'Plenty of veterans who experienced an awful event the way you did, deserted their families when they came back. And plenty of those who stayed, drank and were violent to their wives and children. I don't remember you ever being like that. I think that's admirable. It shows such strength of character, such honour.'

He placed his mug on the table and walked to the window with his back to me. He was silent for a long time. I sipped my Milo. Then he turned around. He looked defeated and so sad I wanted to bite back my words.

'It's hellish. They don't go away, these feelings of guilt. I was never forgiven, you know. Anger boils up so fast; it can be triggered in a second by a sound, a smell, a look. It feels like whatever's happening is aimed just to upset me. That's why I try to keep control of everything, that way I'm ready if something goes awry, I can cope with it.' He leaned his head back and closed his eyes for a moment. When he opened them again he looked me in the eye. I don't know when he ever had before. 'It's exhausting, love. I try to stay in control of everything, everyone around me, just so I don't explode. I've exploded with Mum and you kids too, many times. But if I don't have control over things, this rage escapes before I can catch it. I hate myself for it. I hate myself for killing Joe. The guilt of being alive when he's dead is with me every waking moment.'

'I can't imagine …'

He moved his face closer to mine and again looked me in the eye. 'Don't imagine,' he said in a tense voice, almost a whisper. 'I don't want you to imagine. I don't want you to go anywhere near this. I don't even want us to talk of this. It's my pain, my guilt, not yours. It's none of your business.'

I looked into my cup. 'When I researched your records, it shows that Lieutenant Broom was issued with an AA40 charge. The army found him guilty of neglect in relation to the death of Joe Forrester.' I met his gaze. 'Did you know that? Maybe it wasn't your fault after all. Wasn't Broom supposed to have checked guns at the inspection of arms? Shouldn't he have seen the bullet lodged in the gun? Wasn't it his responsibility? I've read about the Owen and heard other veterans say it was a faulty piece of equipment and often misfired. It's feasible it wasn't your fault at all.'

'I killed Joe, love. I took an innocent man's life – a mate!'

'But Dad, that doesn't make you a bad man. It makes you a victim of the war too – a living victim, suffering through no fault of your own.'

He didn't speak for a long time. He just stared at the tabletop. Had I gone too far? I was thinking of going back to bed, but as I began to get up he started talking again, and his voice had softened.

'I lost my bearings and was set adrift. I lost who I was; I became someone different, yet I was supposed to be the person I was before. When I came back everyone treated me as the before-Jock. But that before-Jock died alongside Joe. I was a different man after the shooting. I didn't know who I was and kept searching for the before-Jock so I could fit in. But I didn't fit in. I don't fit in. I never rest, always on alert, always managing this rumbling inside me.'

He wiped his eyes. He was weeping. My father was weeping.

As I watched him, I thought of how it had been for me as a

child, oblivious to the reasons behind his withdrawal and distance, his frequent outbursts. Now it was obvious to me he was trying to deal with his internal world, but back then, I interpreted it as his lack of interest, his disappointment in me. I think his battle to control his anger prompted me to keep my feelings to myself too. He was always somewhere out of reach, hijacked by the past and too preoccupied to notice my feelings, my world. So my feelings, my world became unimportant.

My heart felt full that he should have expressed his feelings to me. There was nothing more to say to one another, and we sat in silence, in the kitchen, in the early hours of the morning. Neither one of us wanted to move, to break the spell. I don't know how long it was before I heard the faint chirping of a bird – the beginning of the morning chorus.

'I think the sun's coming up,' Dad said.

My first overseas trip was with my mother, father and sister. We sailed on the Sitmar cruise ship, the Castel Felice. This was Dad's first return to the United Kingdom in four decades. He looked proud and happy taking his wife and his two attractive daughters back to his roots. It was to be his only trip. Within three years, he had died. He had one sister left in England, who hadn't immigrated and he was looking forward to seeing her and meeting her family.

The trip back to England was the happiest I'd seen him. He appeared relaxed and open. On the ship, he was a different father to the one at home. Was it because he was in a liminal space again? We had real conversations. Not many but enough. He had the inclination or emotional space to listen and engage in discussion.

My mother was also more peaceful and I remember her looking attractive. As is the case with shipboard life, evenings were a time of dressing up, of glamour. My parents attended a few events and it was the first time I had seen them dancing together. I noticed them walking arm in arm and holding hands. It's hard to imagine your parents being romantic, but I think this trip was a time of rekindling intimacy lost in the day-to-day rhythm of raising five children in a small house. With the luxury of no work, meals cooked and domestic chores taken care of, it looked to me as if my parents' relationship blossomed.

A couple of days out of New Zealand, Dad and I were leaning on the ship's railing, at ease in one another's company. The top of our arms touched just a little. It was sunny and we were looking over the ocean. We chatted about people we had met on the voyage. A sudden, loud gushing noise from a hole in the ship's side surprised us both. Sewage and garbage spewed into the ocean. Brown and grey muck spurted into the silky blue water causing it to turn a murky grey. A flock of seagulls came from nowhere squawking their delight at a ready-made meal. We talked of the environment. I asked him about the future, if every ship did this. He showed interest in my questions. We took turns in thinking of ideas of how to disperse the garbage without polluting the ocean. I can't remember what they were now, but the memory of the two of us resting on the railing is vivid.

He was relaxed on this holiday, possibly reliving old memories before his time at war. When we arrived in the United Kingdom, people made a fuss of him and us. I believe he found pleasure in the familiarity of places, accents, dialects, sights and sounds.

While travelling on the ship and staying at hotels in the United Kingdom, I began to notice educated and interesting people gravitating towards my father. He reciprocated by being charming and engaging in pleasant and interesting conversations. This was a different man from home, where he could be disinterested, rude and detached when people tried to make conversation. I saw my father in a different light. I realised then that he was astute. This was a side of him I hadn't seen before. Possibly, this trait of his personality had always been there and I hadn't seen it. As a teenager, I began to take notice.

*When we returned to Melbourne, we both fell back into old
patterns. I took up with my old friends and wanted more freedom
and independence, and spent as much time as I could away from
my parents. My father returned to his moody, disengaged self.
Within a year, I had left home and within three years he had died.*

I don't know how long he suffered. But it became evident there was
something wrong years before he died. He held the top of his right
arm and took to wearing a faux brown leather glove during the
winter. He said keeping his hand warm helped. It was apparent to
anyone who saw him, he was in pain. During Melbourne's freezing
winters, his face was grey and tense. When he walked, he held his
gloved hand up in front of his chest. No amount of Aspro helped
relieve the mysterious ache in his right arm.

Both Bess and Jock were avid readers and keen library book
borrowers. As far back as I can remember there was a doorstopper
of a Webster's Dictionary on the bookshelf at home. The five-inch-
plus thick *Webster's New Twentieth Century Dictionary of the English
Language Unabridged Second Edition 1960* now rests in the library of
my home. It has a full-page picture of Noah Webster, LLD.

Sniffing the tome takes me back to our lounge room in Preston.

In addition, Jock bought a set of Encyclopaedia Britannica
from a door-to-door salesman. The Webster's Dictionary and the
Encyclopaedia always held a sense of wonderment and strangeness
for me. I enjoyed turning the pages and looking at mysterious
words, trying to work out what they meant. As Jock sat in his chair
next to the bookcase, he often flicked through pages of either the
dictionary or encyclopaedia, stopping to read when something took
his interest. I wonder whether he searched for an understanding
of the way he'd felt since his return to civilian life. Was he looking
for answers to his sadness, depression and rage? Reasons as to why
his right arm ached day and night? Did he think it a coincidence,
or in his heart did he know the pain he carried was feasibly a

manifestation of something else? Psychologists say mysterious pain in the body can be the transference of guilt. This rings true to me in Jock's case.

I often wondered why he didn't seek promotion in his work. He was intelligent, well-respected, well-liked and a good worker, yet he didn't move up from his position as a foreman on the floor. Although not formally educated, he was intelligent and could hold his own in company. His job was to supervise the women who worked on the looms in the factory. Many were Italian migrants who had travelled from their home country in the same way he had. Their English was poor, so Jock taught himself Italian. He often came home with an array of gifts – sugar-coated almonds wrapped in bride's veil, holy pictures in gold frames, homemade cakes and sweets different to the ones we were used to eating.

Aspects of suffering can leave a victim with feelings of inferiority and anxiety. Was this it? Did he prefer to stay safe in his work?

As each child came of age she or he moved out of home. Cleary joined the navy as soon as he was old enough, was stationed in New South Wales and married a Sydney girl. Galvin and Joseph married in their early twenties, had young families of their own and lived in the suburbs of Melbourne. Rose travelled overseas and I moved to Perth to explore the freedom of living in a different city. It was the furthest I could go without needing a passport.

I wondered whether Jock took this personally and thought his children's early departures were due to his mood swings and angry outbursts. His anger had reduced over the years, but he was still emotionally distant.

Bess noticed him becoming more and more tired. His gait had changed. He dragged his feet when he walked. Within minutes of finishing his evening meal he fell asleep in his armchair. The top of his right arm ached throughout his waking hours now and doctors could find no explanation for it.

With just Bess and Jock in the house, without the distractions of children and Jock's full-time work, my parents' closeness from their overseas trip flourished. They took slow short walks of an evening, just to the corner and back, where they held hands or strolled arm in arm as they had done along the foreshore at Eastern Beach. They spent hours chatting together at the kitchen table or sitting in the garden.

Retirement from full-time work, with no responsibilities, didn't improve Jock's health. He was still weary and found it difficult to do much at all. He succumbed to Bess' pleas and visited the doctor.

This time, he was prescribed arthritis painkillers, which took the edge off the pain in his arm, and sent for an array of blood tests. A week later in the doctor's rooms again, Bess knew something was wrong, but the sting of the doctor's words took her breath away. He was diagnosed with leukaemia with six months to live.

Back at the Repatriation Hospital in Heidelberg after nearly three decades, Jock had regular blood transfusions and his bone marrow was checked for leukaemic cells. This time, instead of Bess catching two trains, a tram and a bus, the Department of Veteran Affairs supplied a driver and car for their trips to and from the hospital.

Bess said nothing much had changed from the time she visited Jock in 1945. The coloured lines on the duckboards and the beige walls were the same. But now a photo of the Queen replaced the King's portrait. Bess and Jock made the most of what time they had left. Bess made him comfortable at home and accompanied him to doctors' appointments and blood tests. When he was admitted to the Repatriation Hospital for the last time, he had his own room with an ensuite, and the nurses and doctors were kind and caring. Bess was at the hospital as much as possible and did whatever she could to ensure he was comfortable.

During the last months of Jock's life, there was a stream of visitors. Every few weeks, Honor, Ralph, Tilly and Dorothy drove up from Geelong. Rose and I returned from our travels and we took turns to sit by his bed, sometimes talking, other times just being with him while he slept.

Jock died at around five in the afternoon of 26 April 1973. He was alone. It was one of those indefinite times between visitors. Bess was on her way to see him when he took his last breath just minutes before she arrived. She was heartbroken knowing he had passed away on his own.

The next day, I shopped on the local High Street so there was enough food for people dropping in to pay their respects. Neighbours and a shopkeeper asked after my father. 'He died last night,' I said and watched their faces and discomfort at not knowing what to say or do.

I couldn't understand how life could continue as usual. How people could buy a loaf of bread, chat in the street, sweep the footpath and the gutters in front of their houses when my world had come crashing down around me. Even the light was different. It was too bright for my eyes.

A steady procession of people visited over the days between Dad's death and his funeral. I offered refreshments, scones and slices of cake to family, friends, neighbours, nuns and priests. Grief is exhausting. I've never known such bone-weary tiredness. I could see my mother was exhausted too but found comfort in people visiting. Her grief was too much in those first few days.

She lived in a fog for months.

During the writing of this book, I had a recurring dream.

Jock is in the Repatriation Hospital, sitting up in bed supported by fat hospice pillows, wearing his own green and blue striped pyjamas. The ones he used to wear at home when he sat at the kitchen table to have his breakfast; or when he walked to the front gate of a morning to pick up *The Sun* from the cylinder on top of the letterbox.

The upper button of his pyjama top is undone, exposing three round holes in his chest where the doctors drilled for bone marrow to check his leukaemic cells. The holes looked similar to bullet wounds, with darkened blood caked around the edge of each crater. His eyes are sunken; his face has a grey tinge and is bloated from the cortisone injections. Lank white hair barely hiding his scalp replaces his once thick, curly black mop.

Twenty-two-year-old Joe Forrester walks into the hospital room. He's wearing his army shirt and shorts. Youthful, tanned and lean, he has a bloodied bandage around his head and stands at the foot of Jock's bed. The patient looks up and squints. The late afternoon sun behind Joe makes it difficult to make out who he is.

'Gidday Jock, it's me, Joe.'

'Who?'

'Joe, Joe Forrester.'

Joe sits on the chair by the bed. He leans over and places his hand on Jock's arm. He waits while Jock studies his face.

'I know you thought the shooting was your fault,' Joe said. 'But it was my time to go. I'm sorry you carried the burden for so long.'

Jock begins to cry, quietly at first. Joe moves onto the bed and sits next to him. Jock's body, by now, is wracked with sobs. Joe puts his arm around him.

The older man buries his head in the younger man's chest and cries … for a long time.

My daughter and I finished the cake, and when it was done, we sat under the tree in the garden and ate the first warm slices together. As I daydreamed, wishing Dad could have shared a piece of cake with us, my daughter dropped her fork. The clattering sound it made on the plate made me flinch.

ACKNOWLEDGEMENTS

MANY PEOPLE HAVE CONTRIBUTED to the writing of this book and I am grateful. My thanks go to the numerous veterans and family members of veterans who shared their stories of the impact of living with post-traumatic stress disorder. These stories validated my writing of *Two Generations*. They helped me appreciate how readers are attuned and interested in returned veterans' unacknowledged and untreated PTSD and the impact it has on loved ones – the invisible sufferers.

Thanks and love to Janne Martenengo and David Ward who helped me understand the ramifications of generational suffering and for guiding and supporting me to choose what precious nuggets to keep and what fool's gold to discard.

This book wouldn't have come about without assistance from: the library staff at the Australian War Memorial; Francoise Barr from the Northern Territory Archives Centre – Francoise's guidance and knowledge showed me a thriving Darwin and robust community prior to and during the Japanese bombings; Robert Winther OAM from the Heidelberg Repatriation Hospital; and Reg Elder in the signals section of the Simpson Barracks, Watsonia.

My appreciation extends to Ron Jackson for his generosity of spirit and sharing of information about the brave and colourful men of the 2/14th Australian Field Regiment. His book, *The Broken Eighth – A History of the 2/14th Australian Field Regiment, Darwin – New Guinea – New Britain*, helped me join the dots, bringing to life the lived experience of an Australian soldier in the Second World War. My thanks go to those other gentle, brave and humble men I met from my father's regiment: Tom Adams, Vin Bool, Linc Burchett, Orm Burton and Richard Geeves. Meeting them enabled me to see my father in a new light.

From the broader writing community I am blessed to be affiliated with, I have received only encouragement and support. My thanks go to: Janet Blagg; Lorna Ferguson and Dr John Ballam from the University of Oxford; Babette Smith, Varuna – the National Writers House, the Eleanor Dark Foundation Ltd; my fellow Master-classers, led by Dr Antoni Jach: Gill Barnett, Moreno Giovannoni, Angela Meyer, Janine Mikosza, Anne Myer, Susan Paterson, Patsy Poppenbeck, Honeytree Thomas, Evelyn Tsitas and Clive Wansborough; Lucy Treloar for her mentorship and friendship; Carmel Macdonald Graeme, who has seen me through this book from its infancy. Carmel's gentle feedback and exceptional insight has taught me much about this 'thing' called 'writing'. Karen Throssell for her wealth of knowledge in the written word, encouragement and support. Carmel and Karen have been the midwives of *Two Generations* and I am very grateful.

Big thanks to my agent Sheila Drummond for believing in me, taking me on and managing me and the book through the publishing labyrinth. Thanks to the supportive publishing team: Jane Curry, Eleanor Reader and Zoe Hale.

Appreciation abounds to my family. To Roger Dutton who found the only photograph (to date) of my father with me as a babe. This image is on the front cover of *Two Generations* and has been a strong link to connecting with Jock – so very helpful in delving deeper into the writing. I would like to honour my siblings Mary Connor (deceased), John Connor for his continued enthusiasm and encouragement during the writing, Jim Connor, Elizabeth Ellis and Patrick Connor for his support and having the insight, motivation and patience to record conversations with our mother.

Thanks and love to my daughter Scarlett, for her calm presence, belief and pride in me and to the best son-in-law in the world Tom, for his support.

My deepest gratitude and love to Bernie, for being my chief barracker, for propping me up when I feel a fraud and for everything else.

If I have missed anyone, I am sorry and thank you.

ABOUT THE AUTHOR

Anne Connor is an award-winning Melbourne writer. For over two decades she has worked in the writing space, with articles appearing in *The Age*, *Business Review Weekly* and various lifestyle and industry magazines. Her short stories have been published in anthologies and received awards in short story competitions. Anne headed a marketing and communications consultancy for nine years, and has studied creative writing at Deakin and the University of Oxford. *Two Generations* is her debut memoir.

anneconnor.com.au
anneconnor718@gmail.com

REFERENCES

Alexander, P 1992, 'Australian Pearl Harbor Recalled – Darwin Notes Anniversary of Air Attack', *The Seattle Times*, 19 February.

Alford, B 1991, 'Darwin's Air War, 1942–1945: An Illustrated History', *Aviation History Society of the Northern Territory*.

Birt, G Northern Territory Archives Centre, *Letters from Wartime*, NTAS NTRS 850/P1.

Bridgman D 2006, *The Anglo-asian Bungalow – Housing the Commonwealth Officer in the northern tropics of Australia*, School of Architecture and Design, RMIT University, Melbourne.

Coulthard-Clark, C 2001, *The Encyclopaedia of Australia's Battles*, Allen & Unwin, Sydney.

Daly, M 2003, *Rough Guide to Australia*, Rough Guides, London.

D'Ámbrosio, T 1943, Northern Territory Archives Centre, NTAS, NTRS 226 TS555.

Dash, H 1943, 'Jap Wewak Debacle Death-blow to Lae', *The Courier-Mail*, Brisbane, 19 September.

Dickinson, J 1995, *Refugees in our own Country – The Story of Darwin's Wartime Evacuees*, Darwin Historical Society of the Northern Territory.

Fong Lim, A Northern Territory Archives Centre, Oral Transcript, NTAS 226, TS 211.

Foote, N 2014, *Soldier's Journey to the Top End*, radio program, ABC, 105.7FM Darwin, 14 August.

Forrest, P & S 2012, 'Battle on the Home Front', *NT News*, 18 February, pp. 22–25.

Forster, P Royal Australian Navy, Fixed Naval Defences in Darwin Harbour 1939–1945. Viewed online copy, 3 July 2013.

Frame, T *The Bombing of Darwin*, Quadrant Online. Viewed 2 July 2013.

Fuchida, M & Okumiya, M 1957, *Midway: The Battle that Doomed Japan*, Blue Jacket Books, USA.

Gill, GH 1968, *Royal Australian Navy, 1939–1942. Australia in the War of 1939–1945*. Series 2 – Navy. Australian War Memorial, Canberra.

Gillard, J 2012, 'Darwin Bombing was our Pearl Harbour', *The Age*, Melbourne, 19 February.

Grose P 2011, *An Awkward Truth – the bombing of Darwin February 1942*, Allen & Unwin, Sydney.

Hall, T 1980, *Darwin 1942, Australia's Darkest Hour*, Methuen Australia, NSW.

Harper, WE Northern Territory Archives Centre, Manuscript, NTAS NTRS 275.

Harris, J Northern Territory Archives Centre, Oral Transcript, NTAS NTRS 226, T5843.

Hedges C 2010, *Death of the Liberal Class*, Nation Books, New York City.

Hiromi, T 1997, 'The Japanese Navy's Operations Against Australia in the Second World War, with a Commentary on Japanese Sources'. *Journal of the Australian War Memorial*, Issue 30.

Hughes, RL Northern Territory Archives Centre, War Rations, NTAS NRTS 226, TS 381.

Humble, B Northern Territory Archives Centre, Oral History, NTAS NTRS 226.

Jackson, R 1997, *The Broken Eighth, A History of the 2/14th Australian Field Regiment Darwin-New Guinea-New Britain*, Clipper Press, Melbourne.

Lewis, T 1999, *A War at Home: A Comprehensive Guide to the First Japanese Attacks on Darwin*, Tall Stories, Darwin.

Lockwood, D 1992, *Australia's Pearl Harbour. Darwin 1942*, Penguin Books, Melbourne.

McKernan, M 2001, *This War Never Ends: Australian POWs and Families*, University of Queensland Press, St Lucia.

Medcalf, P 1986, *War in the Shadows, Bougainville 1944–1945*, Collins, Sydney.

O'Brien, K *7.30 Report* 2002, television program, ABC, 19 February.

Powell, A 1983, 'Darwin "Panic", 1942', *Journal of the Australian War Memorial*, 3 October.

Powell, A 1988, *The Shadow's Edge: Australia's Northern War*. Melbourne University Press, Melbourne.

Stanley, P 2002, 'The Bombing of Darwin, 19 February 1942'. *Remembering 1942*, Australian War Memorial.

Stewart, L Northern Territory Archives Centre, NTAS, NTRS 265, All PB191.

Sweet, M 2012, 'How Darwin was Betrayed', *The Age*, February 18.

'The Battle for Darwin' 2012, *Sunday Territorian*, 19 February, pp. 1–30.

The Lowe Report: 1942. Australian War Memorial. Series No AA31, Control Symbol 1949/687.

Tyrell, R Northern Territory Archives Centre, Oral History, NTAS 226, TS 394.

War history. Australian War Memorial, Bombing of Darwin, http://www.awm.gov.au/units/event_59.asp from 19 February 1942 – November 12, 1943. Viewed 2 November 2013.

Wilkshire, J Northern Territory Archives Centre, Oral History NTAS TS 204.

Womack, T Arlington, Texas, http://www.netherlandsnavy.nl/Special_darwin.htm. Viewed 5 December 2013.

Wurth, B 2008, *Australia's Greatest Peril, 1942*. Pan Macmillan Australia, Sydney.

WWII Self-Help Research Tool for Australian Military Records Australia@War.

Websites

The Department of Veterans' Affairs
http://www.dva.gov.au

The Australian War Memorial, 'Remembering 1942: The Bombing of Darwin'
https://www.awm.gov.au/articles/blog/1942-bombing-of-darwin

Australian National University, '*Telling Pacific Lives* free download'
http://press.anu.edu.au//tpl/mobile_devices/ch18.html

Australian War Memorial, 'Gallipoli Ridge Too Far'
http://www.awm.gov.au/blog/2013/04/15/gallipoli-ridge-too-far/
?query=how+many+Australians+and+New+Zealanders+died+at+G
allipoli

Australian War Memorial, 'Second World War'
http://www.awm.gov.au/histories/second_world_war

Sinking of the ship *Zealandia*, in Darwin Harbour on 19th
February, 1942 during a Japanese air attack on Darwin
http://www.ozatwar.com/navy/zealandia.htm

The Parliament of the Commonwealth of Australia, 'Commission of
Inquiry concerning the circumstances connected with the attack
made by Japanese Aircraft at Darwin on 19th February 1942'
http://www.territorystories.nt.gov.au/bitstream/
handle/10070/83913/Lowe_Report.pdf

Australian War Memorial, 'Northern Territory Line of
Communication Area Workshop'
https://www.awm.gov.au/unit/U58124/

Australian War Memorial, 'Journal of the Australian War
Memorial: Issue 30'
http://www.awm.gov.au/journal/j30/tanaka.asp

Australian War Memorial, 'Two Japanese air raids at Darwin, NT
on 19th February, 1942'
http://home.st.net.au/~dunn/darwin02.htm

The Age, 'Darwin bombing was "our Pearl Harbour"': Gillard,
19th February, 1942
http://www.theage.com.au/national/darwin-bombing-was-our-
pearl-harbour-gillard-20120219-1tgr1.html

Quadrant Online, 'The Bombing of Darwin'

http://www.quadrant.org.au/magazine/issue/2009/5/the-bombing-of-darwin

Navy Serving Australia with Pride, 'Fixed Naval defences in Darwin Harbour, 1939–1945'
http://www.navy.gov.au/history/feature-histories/fixed-naval-defences-darwin-harbour-1939–1945

Curtin University, 'John Curtin Prime Ministerial Library'
http://john.curtin.edu.au

National Archives of Australia, 'Your story, our history: The Bombing of Darwin: Fact Sheet 195'
http://www.naa.gov.au/collection/fact-sheets/fs195.aspx